STEAMBOATS
on the Lakes

MAURICE D. SMITH

For Ruth, Romney, Danielle, and Tarragon

STEAMBOATS
on the Lakes

MAURICE D. SMITH

James Lorimer & Company Ltd., Publishers
Toronto

Text Copyright © 2005 Maurice D. Smith
Visual copyright © 2005 James Lorimer & Company Ltd., Publishers

All rights reserved. No part of this book may be reproduced or transmitted in any form or by any means, electronic or mechanical, including photocopying, or by any information storage or retrieval system, without permission in writing from the publisher.

James Lorimer & Company Ltd. acknowledges the support of the Ontario Arts Council. We acknowledge the support of the Government of Canada through the Book Publishing Industry Development Program (BPIDP) for our publishing activities. We acknowledge the support of the Canada Council for the Arts for our publishing program. We acknowledge the support of the Government of Ontario through the Ontario Media Development Corporation's Ontario Book Initiative.

Library and Archives Canada Cataloguing in Publication

Smith, Maurice D.
Steamboats on the Lakes

Maurice D. Smith.

ISBN10: 1-55028-885-7
ISBN13: 978-1-55028-885-8

1. Steamboats—Great Lakes—History. 2. Great Lakes Region—History. I. Title.

HE635.Z7G74   2005   386'.22436'09713   C2005-903949-3

James Lorimer & Company Ltd., Publishers
35 Britain Street
Toronto, Ontario M5A 1R7
www.lorimer.ca

Printed and bound in Canada

Visual credits:
Canada Steamship Lines/John Stobart: p71T
Hamilton Museum of Steam and Technology, p28
Roger LeLievre/BoatNerd.Com: p 77
Walter Lewis: pp 9, 21R, 25, 29L, 30, 31, 37, 41, 52, 68, 69T, 81T
Library and Archives of Canada/George Back, C-093003, p29R
James Lorimer & Company Ltd., Publishers: pp 15, 35
Ian MacAlpine: p79
Marine Museum of the Great Lakes: pp 10, 11R, 11L, 12, 14, 19, 20, 22, 23, 26, 34, 38, 39, 40, 42, 43, 44, 51, 54, 55T, 55B, 56, 57, 58, 59, 61, 62, 63, 65, 66, 70, 71B, 73, 74, 76, 80, 81T. Artists in the Marine Museum Collections: John Charette: p11R; N. Henderson: pp 20, 54; Peter Rindlisbacher: pp 17; E Taylor p 39. For more details contact the author.
Muskoka Steamship & Historical Society Archives: pp 13, 18, 24, 45, 46, 48, 49T, 49R, 50, 60
Ontario Archives: p 2; Ontario Archives/Thomas Burrowes: pp 16, 21T, 32; Ontario Archives/Canadian Pacific Railway Company: p 64; Ontario Archives/M.O. Hammond: p 69B; Ontario Archives/Charles Macnamara: p 47; Ontario Archives/Gordon W. Powley: p 67
Private collection/Peter Rindlisbacher: p 12
Maurice D. Smith: pp 3, 5, 72, 78T, 78B, 81B

Contents

Acknowledgements 6

Preface 7

Chapter 1: The Age of Steam 9
Chapter 2: The Early 19th Century 16
Chapter 3: Canals and the Southern Great Lakes 28
Chapter 4: The Upper Great Lakes 37
Chapter 5: Muskoka 46
Chapter 6: 1880 to the End of World War I 51
Chapter 7: Between the Wars and World War II 56
Chapter 8: After World War II 66
Chapter 9: The Lingering Legacy of Steam 76

List of Ships 82
A Quick Tour of the Ontario Coastline
of the Great Lakes 88
Sources 93
Index 95

ACKNOWLEDGEMENTS

During my museum years I had the distinct pleasure of working as part of a team on a number of special history projects with Walter Lewis, Rick Neilson, Ken Macpherson, Stephen Salmon, and Gordon Shaw, all remarkable marine historians in their own right. Among the Queen's University academics who proved to be very good teachers are Ian McKay, Brian Osborne, and Brian Palmer. John Mills, who worked on his remarkable list of Canadian steamships for well over thirty years, has been generous in making the hard-won results of his research generously available to all. Richard Tatley is the undisputed authority on the marine history of the Muskoka region and the Trent-Severn waterway; James Berry is among the few who have managed a good overview of ships on the American and Canadian side of the Lakes and the history of Georgian Bay; Viktor Kaczkowski gives sense to statistics. Anna Young's *Great Lakes Saga*, published in 1965, is still a useful standby, while the more recent *Steamboat Connections* by Frank Mackey, published in 2000, sets a standard of interpretation and usefulness that most of us can only aspire to. Other works I have listed in the Sources section of this book.

My thanks to the staff at the Queen's University Archives, the Ontario Archives, and the National Archives; to the staff at the main libraries in Hamilton and Toronto, and to the heritage staff in Hamilton. My appreciation also goes to some very diligent MarHst-L subscribers, and to John McKirdy, who generously made available to me the papers of the Thunder Bay Historical Society. My own institution, the Marine Museum of the Great Lakes, has a large collection of primary source material on Great Lakes marine history in the Audrey Rushbrook Memorial Library & Archives. My thanks to the staff of the museum and the Board of Trustees for their support. My appreciation to Francis MacLachlan, who made possible my practical experience at sea and on the Lakes, and to my wife Ruth and my family, who exhibited great patience and understanding. Finally, a thank-you to the publisher, Jim Lorimer, and the production team led by Stacey Curtis, at James Lorimer & Company.

Finally, the perspective is entirely my own, distinctly Canadian, and I take responsibility for that. I have benefited enormously from the work of others.

PREFACE

My interest in Great Lakes maritime history developed over a fourteen-year period while I was in command of the brigantine *Pathfinder*. This fine little vessel took me safely to all of the Lakes except Lake Michigan, and that one I did while aboard an American destroyer, the USS *D.A. Joy*, and on the luxurious *Le Levant* as a lecturer.

There were some close calls aboard *Pathfinder*, particularly on a run up Lake Superior. It was not a dark and stormy night, but late in the afternoon when a sudden fresh breeze and a setting sun, low on the horizon, conspired with a white-out snow squall to reduce our visibility to the length of the ship. It was disorienting in this minimalist swirl of Mother Nature's art, but I forced myself to obey the rule, *trust your compass*. My instincts told me not to. There were no fancy navigation aids for us in the 1960s and '70s but we managed to find refuge in Brule Harbour on the easterly, iron-bound shore of Superior.

Lakes history was a part of every cruise, since the owner of the vessel, Toronto Brigantine Incorporated, was providing leadership training for young sailors. They continue to do so to this day, as does Brigantine Incorporated in Kingston, who have been providing a service aboard ship to youth for well over fifty years. There were other cruises in other parts of the world, but these brigantine days are memorable for me because of the adventure and fine shipmates, many of whom remain valued friends.

There followed a quarter century as the Director and Curator of the Marine Museum of the Great Lakes at Kingston — every day an absolute privilege working with the very stuff of history. This was a period of unmitigated pleasure, consorting with shipowners and shipbuilders, sailors of every rank, museum folk across oceans, and a remarkable group of people who supported the museum through their donation of Canadian history collections, much-needed money, and dedicated volunteerism. Friends remain.

This story deserves more words, but the dictate of the publisher was willingly accepted in the hope others would be encouraged by the breadth of Great Lakes marine history that can only be suggested here. It is my fond hope this book will encourage you to take up the pen and write history. Almost all of us, through family, friends, or place, have a connection with the Great Lakes.

Maurice D. Smith
Kingston, Ontario
July 2005

1

THE AGE OF STEAM

The 19th century was the age of steam technology. In Upper Canada, as Ontario was known until 1841, economic and social development was accelerated by the transport of people and freight by steamboat. The building of two of the Upper Canadian canals, the Rideau and the Welland, was part of a survival strategy to compete with the growing trade and wealth of the United States. A well-placed and timely technology, the steamboat was able to fully exploit the canal system and a natural highway of lakes and rivers that reached into the interior of the province.

The passenger steamship Kingston. *By the beginning of the 20th century, elegant design and fine engineering had produced creations of beauty.*

Although sailing vessels continued to carry low-value bulk cargo into the 20th century, steamboats introduced, probably for the first time in history, the idea of regularity in transportation for the average traveller. Overcoming the limited manoeuvrability of sailing ships, steamboats moved directly into the wind and waves, making predictable progress — most of the time. Passengers could depart from Kingston and travel directly to York, exactly as advertised. It was the steamboat that helped power the transmission of new ideas, political and technological. The arrival of a steamboat at a small wharf at Picton or Port Carling was an event that brought with it news of the outside world. In tandem with the introduction in 1846 of telegraph service between Toronto, Hamilton, Niagara, and St. Catharines, and the proliferation of newspapers, steam transportation helped shrink time and distance. The businessmen and policy makers of the day understood that transportation of people and goods was essential for the survival of Upper Canada, and that government assistance to build the infrastructure was necessary. The British Government undertook

Steamboats on the Lakes

James Watt was a great Scots inventor, engineer, and businessman, whose reputation lives up to his legendary status.

the great public works that helped to keep Upper Canada Canadian — the Upper Canada canals. These were formative years in the development of a Canadian culture and identity. The expectation and acceptance that Canadian parliaments take a social approach to public policy was first established in these 19th-century acts of government support.

It all began with James Watt in Glasgow, Scotland. He started a research and development program in the 1760s and found a partner, Mathew Boulton, to back him financially. The engines manufactured by Boulton and Watt were a great success compared to the previous generation of "atmospheric" steam engines designed by Newcomen. Watt spent the last quarter of the 18th century protecting his patent and improving his machines. The patent ran out in 1800, and the steam engine was then open to further developments, but the reputation of the company persisted. The first steamboat engine in North America, for the *Clermont* in 1807 in the United States, was a Boulton and Watt engine. In 1815, a Watt engine was ordered for the first Upper Canada steamboat, the *Frontenac*. This engine was later passed on to other steamships.

The Age of Steam

 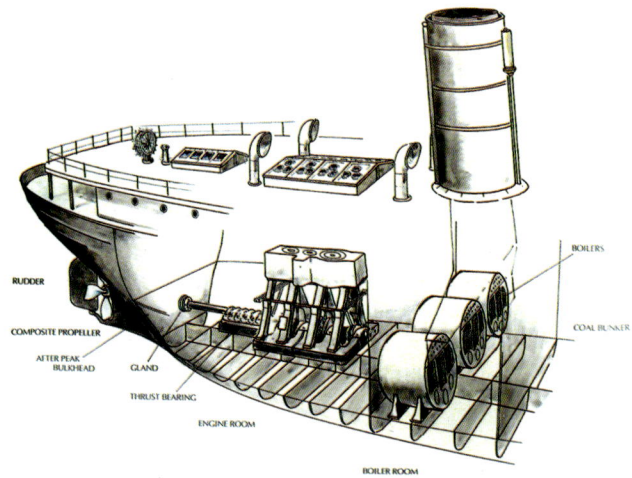

Less than one hundred years separate the primitive walking-beam steam engine of the 1840s (L) and the triple expansion steam engine used on the Lakes bulk carrier of the 1920s.

The principle was simple: light a fire below the water-filled boiler and then use the steam to drive an engine. This simple technology quickly migrated across Upper Canada, making possible industrial centres such as Hamilton, Windsor, and Sault Ste. Marie. Over the course of time, the fuel burned in the boiler firebox changed from wood to coal, followed by oil, and eventually even uranium. At the heart of today's nuclear energy plant is an old-fashioned idea — a steam turbine.

The first steam engines were made out of heavy cast iron and contained a relatively large single piston that operated at a low steam pressure. The hard part was getting the up-and-down motion of the piston rod transferred into the rotary motion needed to turn the paddlewheels on each side of the steamship. The most common solution was a large *walking beam* placed in the upper part of the vessel. The walking beam was moved up and down like a playground teeter-totter by the piston rod attached to one end of the beam. The other end of the walking beam was attached to a rod that rotated a crank attached to the paddlewheel. With two engines, each controlling a paddlewheel, one engine going ahead and the other astern, the vessel could make very tight turns. Unfortunately, since metallurgy was still quite primitive, the metal parts of the steam engines were subject to failure. It was almost impossible to keep the wood hull and superstructure next to the rotating paddles dry. Ice in the spring and floating debris, particularly logs and timber, presented a danger to the exposed paddles.

The paddlewheel steamer was a good choice for rivers and coastal passages where the water was shallow and smooth. The hull was relatively narrow, with the engine and boilers taking up most of the internal space. To increase carrying capacity, a platform was built extending beyond the hull to the outer edge of the paddle boxes on each side of the hull. The platform provided stowage space for freight, and decks above provided room for passengers. Paddlewheel steamships were in use well into the 20th century, but

The Brig Liverpool. *Sailing vessels competed effectively with steamships for many years as, size for size, they could carry more cargo.*

almost exclusively for the passenger trade in protected waters. By then the engines and controls were far more sophisticated, and hulls were made of riveted iron or steel and thus more watertight.

Remembered in song and story, Great Lakes shipwrecks number well over 5,000. Shipwreck divers can easily determine where the wrecks are located. The strongest winds are from the west and northwest. Gales are common in late October and November. If the wind and sea were strong enough, a sailing vessel or low-powered steamship had little choice but to run in the direction of the wind. On Lake Ontario, look to the west side of Prince Edward County for shipwrecks and a shoreline that had to be rounded before reaching the safety of Kingston. On Lake Erie, Point Pelee and Long Point sucked up ships. In rain and at night, these low, sandy points disappeared, and the only warning a captain might hear was "Breakers ahead!" before he ran up on to a lonely beach. On Lake Huron, the upper part of the Bruce Peninsula and the string of islands and shoals between Tobermory and Manitoulin Island were the sites of many shipwrecks, with little chance of rescue for the crew. All of Lake Superior was treacherous. The worst of Lake Michigan was from the Sleeping Bear Dunes to the Mackinaw. And, on any of the Lakes, when the wind changed and blew strong out of the east, all of the rules changed.

Human error, whether through fatigue or stupidity, accounts for some losses, and boiler explosions led in 1859 to the requirement that steam engineers have certification. But most early sailors who learned by experience were very good at their trade. They started at a young age, and only the most competent would be entrusted by shipowners to command a vessel. Most sailors had learned their skills in the best school available — the sailing ship. Because of the seamanship, teamwork, and knowledge of the weather needed to sail these vessels, the tall ship is still used for training today.

Some ships simply fell apart. It was almost impossible to keep a wood hull, built out of hundreds of pieces of wood in constant compression and tension, watertight for any length of time. As one sailor told me, "There is them that leaks and thems that do not leak as much." Ships, sail and steam, were frequently overloaded, sometimes with cargo the hull was not designed to carry. With the added weight of machinery, an early steamship could be an accident waiting to happen. The hull narrowed and as a result there

The steam gauge — a safety device introduced to help prevent boiler explosions.

was not enough buoyancy to support the weight of cargo placed at the ends of the hull. This caused a defect called sagging, as the bow and stern drooped. The Egyptians had the same problem with their vessels thousands of years ago. To counteract this, the sidewheel steamboat designers copied the Egyptians and placed high posts at a point between the bow and stern, and then ran cables forward and aft to hold up the ends. In time the support system became more elaborate, making the steamboats look like old-fashioned road bridges.

A few bad years of trade would often lead to poor maintenance, which further increased the danger. Discussions of why shipwrecks occurred often included criticism of the innate conservatism of mariners, their unwillingness to accept "improvements," but there was a good reason why sailors were reluctant to change things: the sailoring trade was dangerous and new ideas were frequently untested. A ship away from port was on its own, as were the sailors, who liked what they knew they could depend upon.

For the passenger, the worst feature of a sailing ship was its reliance on the wind for power. Becalmed, the ship did not move. With too much wind, the sailing vessel could go only the way the wind blew, often onto an inhospitable beach. Light winds slowed progress down to a drift that easily led to frustrating hours with a harbour in sight and no way to get there. And then, if an offshore wind came up, more hours were spent zigzagging towards the objective. The sailing ship was nearly always a cargo carrier with passengers carried on deck or, for the

Steamboats on the Lakes

The first and most effective bulk carriers were rafts built to transport timber and goods from Upper Canada down the St. Lawrence River towards Quebec City.

privileged, in a house built on the deck. Even the best quarters were cramped, and there was no room for privacy. There were no toilets, of course; men could "go" over the side, remembering the simple wisdom to never aim into the wind. In a heavy sea, the decks heaving and never level, women had to wedge themselves and their chamber pots into a tight corner to manage their ablutions. In heavy weather the simple act of eating a meal required the agility of a contortionist. In gale-force winds, galleys were closed down because of the danger of starting a fire. A friendly "front of house" staff did not exist; the captain and sailors were more concerned with sailing the ship.

And then, losses such as this wreck on Lake Ontario in 1876, memorialized in song, were part of the public imagination:

So dusk came down the darkness next, it was a fearful night,
The ill-fated Maggie Hunter, she's now far out of sight,
She's now far out of sight, my boys, now will be seen no more,
Down in the deep now all do sleep far from their friends on shore.
Six months afterwards the cook was found floating near the shore,
The many friends that loved her will never greet her more,
A hatch, a boom, a broken spar, the drowned woman's pale dead face,
Of that stout craft and gallant crew remained the only trace.

No wonder passengers quickly embraced the steamship as a way to travel. They much preferred the new over the old. A simple passage from Kingston to Toronto with a contrary wind might take three days; in steam, only a day. The danger and discomfort of a steamship was far less than that of a sailing ship.

The Great Lakes were surveyed in the early 19th century, but charts were not generally available until much later. Many places were re-surveyed in the 1880s, once the substantial increase in the number and value of steel steamships and correspondingly large losses of life forced governments to respond to the need for more and better lighthouses and channel markers. The same conditions led to the introduction of formal training for officers. Loss of life was frequently needed to get a "squeaky wheel" noticed or to get safety-related legislation passed. The real success is that there were so few lives lost considering the thousands of passages made by individuals who took their skills and the horrific risk for granted as part of the job. Steam technology, daring entrepreneurs, rough sailors, and a good mix of politics and nationalism mark the age of steam and the story of the growth of Ontario.

A look at a map of Ontario sets the scene: Upper Canada was almost surrounded by water. The most obvious waterways are four of the five Great Lakes: Ontario, Erie, Huron, and Superior. The Ottawa River is the boundary between Ontario and Quebec, while the St. Lawrence River and the Great Lakes mark the boundary with the United States. In the north, the Ontario shoreline runs along a good part of Hudson Bay and James Bay. And yet with all of these water transportation resources, Upper Canada was a colony cut off from itself. The great rivers and lakes were both highways and roadblocks. Rapids on the St. Lawrence River between Prescott and Montreal held back Upper Canada's economic development and prevented effective communication with the rest of

Ontario, with its 250,000 lakes and over 100,000 kilometres of rivers, deserves to be called a maritime province.

the world until the mid-19th century. The height of the "great cataract," Niagara Falls, had to be overcome before Lake Ontario and Lake Erie could be linked by the Welland Canal. There were roads, but they were primitive, and many would not be improved until well after World War II. The railways would be the only efficient land transport, but did not fully compete in the carrying of bulk goods until well into the 20th century. Ships are still, in the 21st century, the most cost-effective way, per ton mile, to move goods.

2

THE EARLY 19TH CENTURY

Lake Ontario was the cradle of steam-powered ships in Ontario. It was also the hard-headed, no-quarter-given nursery of men who would try every imaginable business configuration to force entrepreneurial growth. Over the decades, the steamship companies, which evolved from uncomplicated sole proprietorships or partnerships to limited liability companies to, finally, huge conglomerates at the beginning of the 20th century, were important organizational ventures that moved in step with technological progress and access to investment capital. It is no accident that, just as developing technology enabled increased steam pressure in boilers and more powerful engines, so did business opportunities expand for developing new markets. To the south, the United States was exercising its new muscles and, as always, the Canadian response was an imaginative, no-frills variant. For the first half of the century, British policy encouraged trade with the colonies. Through a few political favours for friends of the government, a bit of money made available, and new legislation, the colony

Opinicon Lake looking to the NW, *1840. The early steamboats faced many challenges, not the least being uncharted waters full of obstacles.*

The Early 19th Century

The Glorious Age of Sail & Steam. *Only sixty years separates the full flowering of sail and steam from the launch of the Frontenac in 1816.*

was able to survive, to build steamships — British *bottoms* to carry colonial goods — and to keep a colony, almost empty of people, safe for England.

Commercial investors gathered quickly on both sides of the border after the War of 1812. Still fresh in the memories of both the British colonists and the Americans was the enormous difficulty they'd had in moving war supplies. Compared to cross-country travel through barely penetrable forests and swamps, movement by water was easy, even if it was by sail, oars, or paddle. Nonetheless, it took two to three days to sail from Kingston to York (Toronto) and if the wind was out of the west, which it frequently was, the passage could be wet, crowded, cold, and at an angle of heel that prevented that most ordinary of on-deck activities, walking upright. Summer breezes were lighter and easier on the stomach, but made schooner and brig passages slower.

Progress had been made in the development of a sailing ship rig for inland waters. The first sailing vessels on the lakes were almost copies of those used in the coastal areas of Europe and the United States, and on the oceans of the world. The use of square sails, common at sea, was mostly eliminated due to the weather conditions on the Lakes, the labour needed to operate them, and the constant proximity of shore. The Great Lakes schooner emerged and evolved into a Lakes type that survived into the 20th century. The two-master and the "Three 'N' Afters," their decks loaded down to the gunwale with cargo and carrying a lofty rig of sails, were the ultimate expression of human ability to work in concert with wind and wave — and to be smart about it. These ships were powered by a combination of technological ingenuity and the whims of nature, with its "no wind" one day and "a gale, me boys" the next. And that was the problem. Up to the moment steamboats appeared, Mother

Steamboats on the Lakes

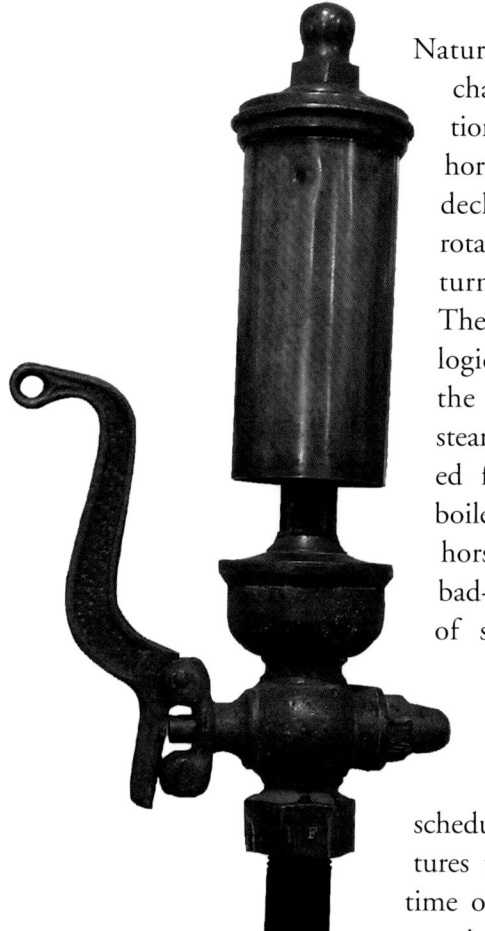

The sound of the whistle at the dock signalled the arrival of letters, supplies, new faces and friends, and news of the outside world.

Nature was in complete charge, with one exception, the horse ferry. The horse walked in a circle on deck or on a treadmill, rotating a set of gears that turned the paddlewheels. The horse ferry was technologically midway between the sailing ship and the steamboat. The horse needed fuel, just like a steam boiler, and after a while, the horses went mad or just bad-tempered. The promise of steam-boats, especially liked by passengers, was speed, less time on the water, and a far more predictable schedule of arrivals and departures than sailing ships. Less time on the water meant less time exposed to danger.

In 1815, investors at Kingston, hearing of plans to build a steamship on the American side of the Lakes, moved quickly. The merchants did not like the possibility of their former enemies capturing trade on the Upper Canadian shore of Lake Ontario. After receiving a secret military evaluation in 1815, British officials easily saw the advantage of building steamboats. They remembered how difficult it was during the War of 1812 to move critical war supplies using oars, sails, and ox teams to haul the boats. Now the difficulty for the steam promoters was finding money. There simply were not enough people living in Upper Canada to provide investment capital. Kingston was the leading centre, with a population of 2,400. York, Queenston, and Niagara-on-the-Lake had, combined, about the same number of settlers as Kingston, but these locations had suffered as battlegrounds during the war and hadn't the resources to invest. The available pool of investors in Upper Canada was limited. Kingston merchants took the lead in buying shares. The only restriction was designed to keep the Americans out: "No Alien shall hold a Share in the Boat either by Subscription purchase, or transfer."

By October of that year, 1815, the Kingston investors had raised the money and made a critical decision: not to re-invent the wheel, so to speak, but instead to base their engine specifications and hull design on the *Car of Commerce*, launched in Montreal earlier in the month. Boulton and Watt, located in Birmingham, England, were chosen to build the engines. The company was a logical choice, since they had supplied the engine for the first American steamship to ply the Hudson River, the *Robert Fulton*, built in 1807. The first Canadian steamboat, *Accommodation*, built by beer magnate John Molson in 1809, was the first steamboat to be built entirely in North America, including the engines. Its Canadian-built engines were not entirely satisfactory, so Molson used Boulton and Watt engines for his second steamboat, the *Swiftsure*, built in 1812. The reputation of the English builders was secure — for the moment.

Ships throughout most of the 19th century were made of large pieces of wood, and in Ontario there

The Early 19th Century

Early steamships were built of wood and burned wood fuel. The Kingston, *built in 1852, suffered the fate of many steamships — loss by fire.*

was an abundance of supply. Good oak was available, along with pine and ash. A wood-ship–building yard could be set up on almost any shoreline as long as the water was deep enough to launch the ship. Hand carpentry, a blacksmith shop, and horses were among the pre-industrial resources needed. The technology for building wooden sailing ships was well understood, but the building of the first steel ship in Ontario decades later, in 1889, was full of complexity, requiring advanced organizational and worker skills yet to be invented in 1816. Lessons in building steamships were still to be learned. A massive iron engine with heavy, moving parts produced a new set of stresses in a wooden hull. Placing a wood-fired boiler in the middle of a wooden ship was often a fiery accident waiting to happen — and it did — picturesquely described in 19th-century accounts as a conflagration. The first vessels built for the Lower St. Lawrence River, the *Accommodation*, *Swiftsure*, and *Malsham*, all for John Molson, were early efforts or prototypes, each not lasting more than a few years. The *Car of Commerce*, the model for the *Frontenac*, was a little more long-lived, lasting seven years; in retrospect, it turned out to be as good a design as could be hoped for by the ambitious builders in Kingston.

In their anxiety to be first, to beat the Americans, the Kingston promoters hired American builders Henry Teabout and James Chapman, former enemies during the War of 1812 from just across the Lake, to build the *Frontenac*. The wood was assembled at the building site at Finkle's Point near Ernestown (now Bath) and inspected, the keel was laid in early 1816, and by September, following months of miserable weather including snow in June, the *Frontenac* was

In service by 1817, the Frontenac *was the largest steamship on the Lakes at the time.*

finally ready. The *Kingston Gazette* reported on the launching.

> On Saturday the 7th of September, the Steam Boat FRONTENAC was launched at the village of Ernest Town. A numerous concourse of people assembled on the occasion. But in consequence of some accidental delay, and the appearance of an approaching shower, a part of the spectators withdrew before the launch actually took place. The boat moved slowly from her place, and descended with majestic sweep into her proper element. The length of her keel is 150 feet; her deck, 173 feet. Her proportions strike the eye very agreeably; and good judges have pronounced this to be the best piece of naval architecture of the kind yet produced in America. It reflects honor upon Messrs. Teabout & Chapman, from New York, the contractors, and their workmen, and also upon the proprietors, the greater part of whom are among the most respectable merchants and other inhabitants of the County of Frontenac, from which the name is derived.

The newspaper reporter was cautious. "Steam navigation having succeeded to admiration on various rivers, the application of it to the waters of the Lakes is an interesting experiment." Building the *Frontenac* was a daring, gutsy venture. *Frontenac* was substantially larger than her rival, the *Ontario* out of Sackets Harbour, New York. She was also the largest commercial vessel built on the Lakes, at a cost of £7,000.

On this maiden passage *Frontenac* was moved from Ernestown to Kingston using wind power. Like all early steamships, she was equipped with masts and sails, a kind of insurance policy in the event of an engine breakdown. They were reassuring for passengers and, when the wind was in the right direction, sails were set to assist the engines and reduce fuel costs. *Frontenac's* first voyage under steam was on May 23, 1817, a month after that of her American rival, the *Ontario*. The *Frontenac* was first to launch, second to use engines — but first to take to the water.

Henry Gildersleeve, a Kingston resident, had the good fortune to be in on the building of the *Frontenac*. On the same site he built and launched the *Charlotte*, one year later in 1818. The *Charlotte* ran between Prescott and Carrying Place on the Bay of Quinte for nine years, a compliment to Gildersleeve's fine business sense. This was a bread-and-butter run, more like a delivery van than a thirty-wheeler rolling down the 401 highway. The *Charlotte* was 130 feet long and only 18 feet wide, with engines installed by John Dod Ward. The critical dimension, the depth of hold, was 8 feet, which meant the amount of hull in the water was less. These dimensions were ideal for smallish harbours like Picton and Trenton, and for a

The Early 19th Century

busy harbour like Kingston. Early in his career, Gildersleeve showed good business sense, matching the size of steamship with the route and recognizing places that needed to be connected by water in the small-town atmosphere of the province at the time. Immigrants had to be carried west from Prescott to Carrying Place near Trenton, where they were transferred a short distance overland to another ship waiting in Presqu'ile Bay at the east end of Lake Ontario. Many of these travellers had escaped the privations of England to take up farming or a trade north and west of Toronto. Local villagers and farmers used the *Charlotte* to ship produce or just go visiting other towns along the route.

The *Frontenac* was intended as a riverboat for passengers and freight between Prescott and Kingston. On that first commercial run to Prescott she touched bottom. That was enough to send *Frontenac* into the deeper waters of Lake Ontario where, with fewer shoals, the owners thought she would be safer. The round-trip fare in cabin class from Kingston to York was eighteen dollars; it was twelve dollars for one way. There were rules, and decorum had to be maintained:

Top: The Bay of Quinte, with its protected waters, was an ideal and safe place to operate colonial steamboats. The one shown here wears the red ensign, later known in the marine world as the red duster. *Bottom:* The *Charlotte* demonstrated that the owner Henry Gildersleeve understood steamboat design in the early days of his business.

"Gentlemen's servants cannot eat in cabins. No smoking allowed in the cabin nor any gentleman allowed to visit the Ladies' Cabin without special permission." One traveller, John Howison, was full of gratitude. "I could not but invoke a thousand blessings on the inventors and improvers of the steamboat for the delightful mode of conveyance with which

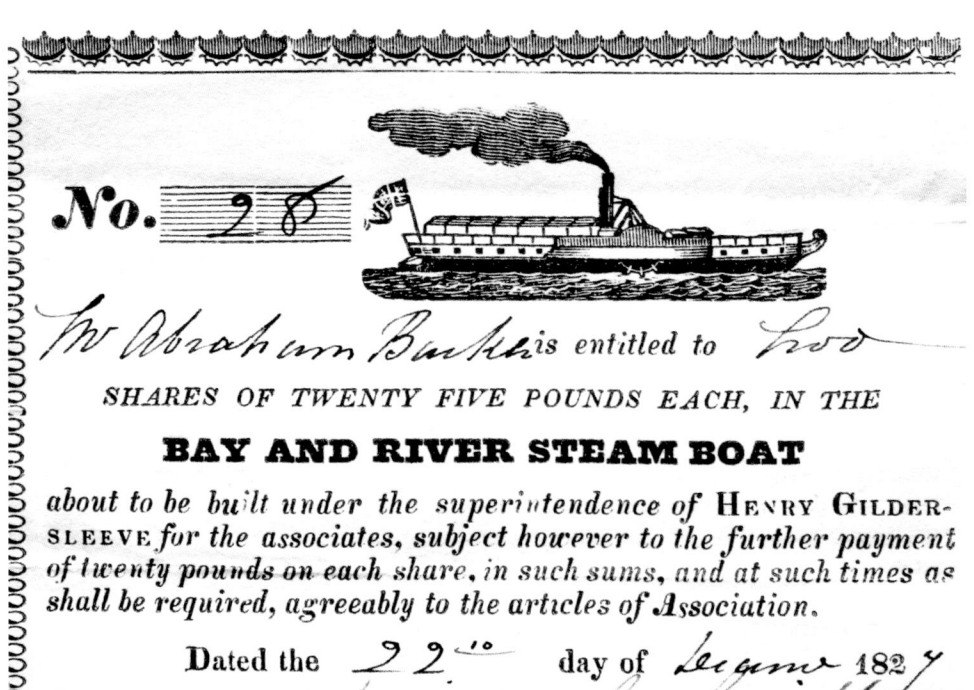

A share certificate issued to raise funds to build a Bay and River Boat. Henry Gildersleeve was to superintend the building.

good memory and experience of a captain and mates were of more value to navigation than the rudimentary charts. At 50 horsepower, the *Frontenac* was grossly underpowered for her size. She could take longer to move from Kingston to York than sailing vessels, yet she persisted until 1827. Afterwards she caught fire in the Niagara River. The steamship *Niagara* towed her to a beach to save the iron in her. The engines were removed for later use in the *Alciope*, and still later in the *Adelaide*, the first Canadian steamship on Lake Erie.

John Hamilton purchased the *Frontenac* in 1825. He came into his inheritance in 1824 while working as a merchant's clerk in Montreal, a position that not only provided good business training but was ideal for making contacts. He qualified in every way as a member of the landed gentry — his family had extensive holdings in Upper Canada. He and his brother Robert purchased the *Frontenac*, ran it for two years, then stripped it of the still-valuable Boulton and Watt engine for use in other boats.

By the early 1830s John Hamilton had built the *Great Britain* in Prescott for £20,000. She was big — 147 feet long with two engines built by Bennett & Henderson in Montreal — and designed to carry

their labours have been the means of furnishing mankind. It required some recollections to perceive I was not in the Kingston Hotel." Travelling steerage class was cheaper, at three dollars; passengers could bring their own food or "be furnished by the steward." The alternative, stagecoach travel, was described by Sir Richard Bonnycastle before mid-century as a journey marked by "mud-holes that would astonish a cockney…and rough places enough to dislocate every joint in your body." The preference many had, to walk between Kingston and York, is understandable.

Frontenac remained under the command of Captain Mackenzie for her ten-year career. In 1817 the

The Early 19th Century

The Great Britain *was popular with passengers due to its size, stability, and powerful engines.*

mail, passengers, and freight on Lake Ontario. The combination of length and weight with lots of power was to cause problems. The engines and connecting parts were made out of cast iron that had hidden defects (not uncommon in the early days of metallurgy) and as a result there were three breakdowns over the last half of her active career. The solid hull was only 23 feet wide, but when a paddle box was added on either side, the width nearly tripled to "about 60" feet. *Great Britain* was very popular with passengers, who probably found her very stable for her size, and with merchants who used her for freight. One passenger described her as having "as many conveniences as a fashionable hotel. The cabins are long and broad and furnished in the most sumptuous manner — that appropriated to the use of the ladies has sofas, mirrors and every other luxury." John Hamilton was owner of many ships, among them the *Canada, Lord Sydenham, Magnet,* and *Passport.*

The building and the operation of the *Frontenac* was full of first-time lessons that were closely observed. Steam engineers who had an exclusive understanding of their engines were, at first, a kind of secret fraternity. They were not above telling captains how to operate their ships until that power relationship was firmly sorted out in favour of captains.

Lighthouse and harbour charges were levied by governments and so seriously reduced profits that owners had to learn how to exert political pressure for their own interests. Shipbuilders had to design a new kind of strengthened hull, and engineers, a different propulsion system. Simple blacksmithing suitable for sailing-ship rigging evolved into local machine shops and foundries so engines didn't need to be imported but could be built in Upper Canada instead. Building steam engines for use on the Lakes was not as simple a matter as just copying what had been done on the St. Lawrence River, in England, or in the United States. Operators of Lakes steamships could not just rely on poaching experienced men, as the promoters of the *Frontenac* had done when they recruited John Leys from Boulton and Watt in England. Lake Ontario, more like a small inland sea than a lake, was a distinctive place for operating steamships — as could be said about many another body of water across North America or Europe. Each body of water has its own distinctive wind systems, currents, shorelines, and harbours. The best ships were those designed for the waters they sailed in.

The push to build business empires and, along the way, improve the technology came from entrepreneurs, hard-headed businessmen who knew how to find money and, on a day-to-day basis, engage in a cut-throat competitive business. The lives of the steamboat owners who dominated the upper St. Lawrence River and Lake Ontario intersected at many levels. Gildersleeve, built and operated many ships, including *William IV* (1831), the *City of Kingston* (1847), *Commodore Barrie* (1834), the *Prince of Wales* (1841), and the *New Era* (1848). By the names of his ships there was never any doubt about his allegiance to the British crown. The *New Era* was no doubt in celebration of the opening of the St. Lawrence Canal from Lake Ontario to Montreal and on to the sea.

Donald Bethune, born in 1802, was a politician and lawyer who saw an opportunity in shipping while in the midst of a career in banking. He launched his first steamboat, the *Britannia*, at Kingston in late 1832. She was outfitted with twenty-six cabins for men and sixteen for ladies — a very tight squeeze for

The weigh scales helped settle the fee charged to carry cargo.

The Early 19th Century

The success of the Shickluna Shipyard at St. Catharines was due to the prosperity of successive ship owners and the early year growth of the province.

a 109-foot ship. The "cabins" were narrow, really just tiny cubicles with barely a place to sleep, and no doubt the atmosphere was rather heavy each morning with so many chamber pots to empty. Two years after the launch of *Britannia*, Bethune was in financial trouble, but he bounced back. By 1846 he decided to take on his only real competitor in a price war. One observer said, "Bethune and Richardson I look upon as gone loons…they are now running against each other to their mutual destruction." The competitor, Hugh Richardson, truly one of the good guys, went bankrupt. Bethune followed in 1848.

Love or hate them, these men were full of character. Richardson was held a prisoner of war in France for eight years after serving with distinction at sea with the Royal Navy. He arrived in Canada in 1821. His first steamer, the *Canada*, was built in 1825 and he managed to stay in business until 1847. In 1832, going through bad times, he said, "Sink I often think I shall — founder in the midst of a mine of gold, with a millstone about my neck." He was often in debt but, unlike his nemesis, the dastardly Bethune, he met his obligations. Among his other ships were the *Queen Victoria*, the very popular *Chief Justice Robinson*, and the *Transit*.

Neither Bethune's bank nor his many creditors along the north shore of Lake Ontario could afford to cast him adrift. He repaid them by skipping town in 1853 with £4,000. Bethune had talent. Among his ships were the *America*, the *City of Hamilton*, and the *Commerce*. One of the most famous was the 170-foot *Maple Leaf*, built in Kingston in 1851. She left Canada in 1862 for service with the Union Army during the American Civil War. She was sunk by a Confederate torpedo near Jacksonville, Florida, and is now one of the most important American Civil War archaeological sites.

The game of shipowning was like gambling — strong winds, heavy waves, and surviving "dark and stormy nights" were like the roll of the dice or the turn of a card. Alliances were made and then broken. Old enemies became friends. A steamship route would be established, say, from Prescott to Kingston, and then a competitor's steamships would be put in opposition. A price war would break out between two shipowners and a third would retire to a different route to survive, and then, like John Hamilton, bounce back again. In the early 1840s, Hamilton made a "tactical advance to the rear." He let Donald

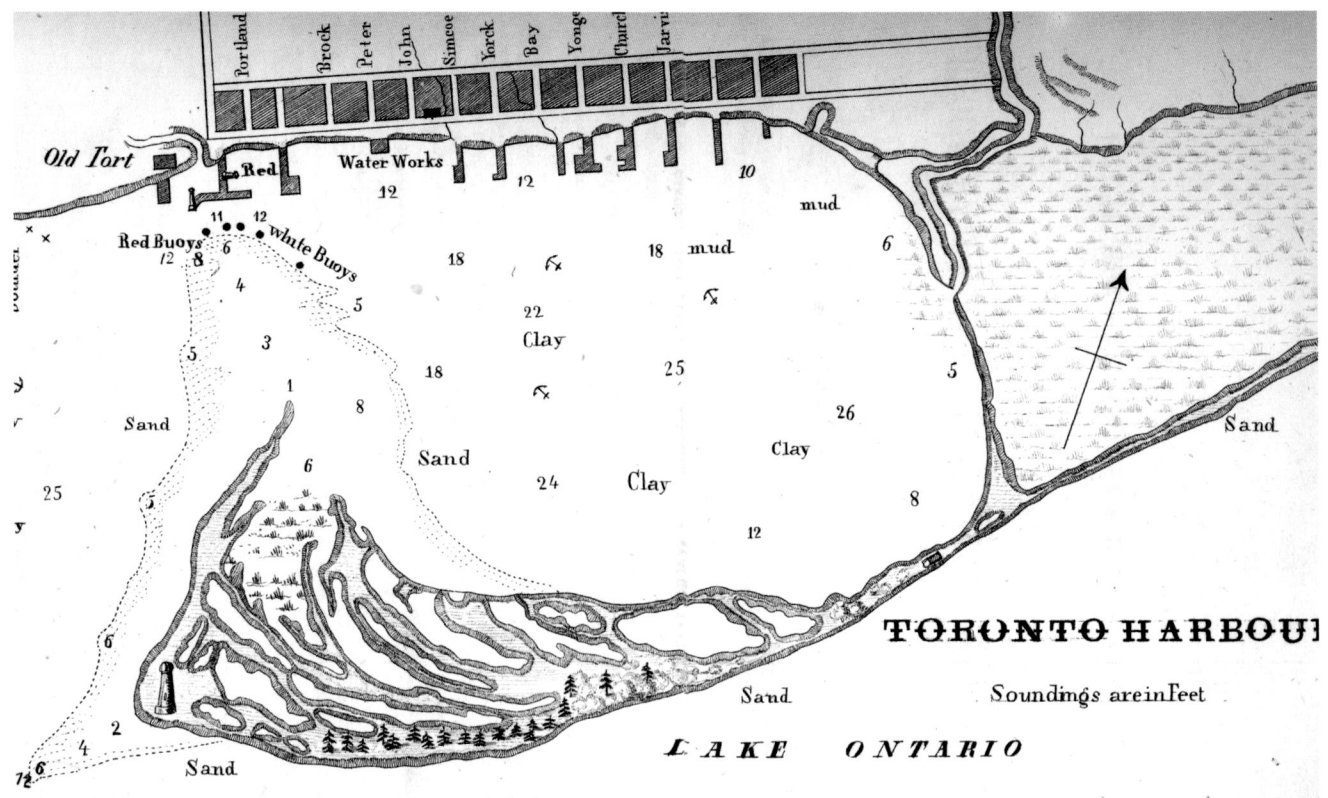

Toronto Harbour chart, 1857. Hugh Richardson, steamship owner and first Toronto Harbourmaster, was devoted to the development of the city's harbour.

Bethune and Hugh Richardson battle it out to ruin on Lake Ontario while he concentrated on the St. Lawrence River route — in 1850 he returned to Lake Ontario. Driven into bankruptcy in 1861 by the railways and bad business conditions, he bounced back to a shipping partnership in 1865 and another Royal Mail line. As a banker he found it easy to call in the detested Bethune's loan.

These four shipowners stand out from the rest in the formative decades leading up to the middle of the 19th century.

John Hamilton and Henry Gildersleeve were solid characters who made long lasting contributions to the community. In a century when most men were worn out at fifty, Henry Gildersleeve, at sixty-three, was the founder of a shipping dynasty that would carry on after him. He had been a ship's captain, a shipbuilder, and a businessman, "well known for the urbanity of his manners." He was an optimist, a conciliator, willing to negotiate with competitors, to come to arrangements that would benefit both. He built a fine house in Kingston in 1825 that is still there, and his many admirers describe him as the "father of steam navigation on the Great Lakes."

John Hamilton had an almost continuous political career from 1831 to 1867 as a legislator, and then in

The Early 19th Century

1867 became a Senator in the new Canadian Parliament. He exploited — honourably, for the 19th century — all the opportunities that came his way, through family, politics, business networks, and banking. He was a strong Presbyterian, a friend of Sir John A. Macdonald, a co-founder of Queen's University, and father to ten children.

Hugh Richardson was a bit of a hothead, but admirable; the other, Donald Bethune, was a successful crook. Richardson ended his career a fine old man, surrounded by friends, as the first harbourmaster for the city of Toronto (as York had been renamed in 1834) and he made improvements to his beloved harbour. He was of "chivalrous temperament" and his looks matched his character. Bethune returned from England in 1858, settled down in the small town of Port Hope to practise law, and by 1864 was doing well. He eventually became a Queen's Counsel. He had the gift of the gab, always getting credit from banks and relations, and always in debt. Many knew him as an accomplished lawyer, but others saw him as a corrosive character who took good people down. Fair representation here: in these men, Gildersleeve, Hamilton, Richardson, and Bethune, it is easy to recognize the characteristics, good and bad, of businessmen at the beginning of the 21st century.

Aristocratic passengers visiting from England in the 19th century were shocked with the jostle of humanity ashore and the roughness of vendors on the dock. Bonnycastle was "jostled almost into the water by rude carters plying for hire on the narrow bounds, and pestered by crowds of equally rude pliers for hotel preference." The man on the street was cocky, always eager to challenge those who stood on rank and privilege; egalitarianism was in the air. The English author Charles Dickens had a more benign experience in 1841:

The time of leaving Toronto for Kingston is noon. By eight o'clock next morning, the traveller is at the end of his journey, which is performed by steamboat upon Lake Ontario, calling at Port Hope and Coburg, the latter a cheerful, thriving little town. Vast quantities of flour form the chief item in the freight of these vessels. We had no fewer than one thousand and eighty barrels on board, between Coburg and Kingston.

By the early 1840s, the province was filling up with people. Many farms were productive enough to develop an export trade. At the same time, the disruptions caused by the Upper Canada rebellions and a depression, both at the end of the 1830s, were receding. Shipowners had reason to be optimistic. Upper Canada was being populated and the natural barriers between the sea and other Lakes were being eliminated by the construction of canals and locks. The first half of the century needed men like Hamilton, Gildersleeve, Bethune, and Richardson. They were pioneers, but in the 1860s a development took place that even they would have trouble coping with. The railways were gaining in strength. In the years ahead, railways and steamships were co-dependent, at times entering into uneasy alliances.

3

CANALS AND THE SOUTHERN GREAT LAKES

The Magnet. *This remarkable steamship, built in 1847, outlived the 19th century.*

The late 1830s and early 1840s were troublesome years in British North America. The anger of the people expressed itself in a range of ways, from simple protests arguing for self-government to a bloody rebellion in Lower Canada where British troops gunned down and burned protestors. In Upper Canada, the British-appointed governor and executive council ruled the colony, doling out favours to their elite friends, an arrangement Reformers called the Family Compact. The 1837 Rebellion and the years that followed created an uncertain business climate in a colony where investment money was already in short supply. These were also the years in which big ideas, such as representative government, took root. There were projects to put into place a transportation system that would allow effective water transportation between the oceans and Lake Superior. Sailing ships dominated

Canals and the Southern Great Lakes

The Walk in the Water, *the first vessel to be launched on Lake Erie. The first Canadian steamboat followed in 1832. In terms of water transportation, Erie was an American lake.*

The Kakebeka Falls were among the many natural obstacles that had to be faced by fur traders.

the seas of the world and the Great Lakes well into the 19th century. In the 1820s and '30s, steamboats caught the imagination of British thinkers and planners looking to the future.

Officials on both sides of the Atlantic were running scared in the early years of the colony of Canada. The competition from the United States was brutal and efficient, forcing them to move as fast as possible to protect their remaining British colonies. The outstanding commercial success of the American Erie Canal in 1825 opened up Atlantic ports, such as New York, to the Great Lakes. The Erie immediately drew trade away from Montreal and the St. Lawrence River route. The cost of shipping goods from New York City to Buffalo dropped 90%, and many immigrants preferred to travel by canal boat between these two cities to start the safer and more comfortable American route into the western states.

The cycle of the seasons in Upper Canada was unlike anything experienced by Europeans. Winters isolated pockets of people for months. The unprepared died. The shoreline waters of even the largest of the Great Lakes froze in the winter. The spring brought melting snow and rain, mud and insects, making it seem that the plagues visited upon the Egyptians by Moses had reappeared in Upper Canada. Corduroy and dirt roads were impassable, while rivers in full flood were too dangerous. The best time for land travel was in the dry summers and fall — and, surprisingly, in the deep winter. Local roads were pushed through the bush and around hills and swamps, but these roads, even though improved over the years, were inadequate to carry cargo in bulk. The obvious answer was to use the existing waterways, the Great Lakes and connecting rivers that reached to the interior of the continent.

The rapids on the St. Lawrence River prevented free movement of ships into and out of Upper Canada. It seemed a miracle that anything happened at all in such a sparsely populated place. Money needed for improvements had to be borrowed from investors in England. The economy was stalled; not enough people, cash, or credit. Barter or trade was the best option for exchanging goods. The farmland easily demanded the full working life of a generation of settlers before the tree stumps disappeared from the fields and left enough space to plant a crop of grain. And yet the colonists were productive. By the 1840s, wheat was an export crop. The challenge was to build a transportation system that broke down the natural barriers, connected all the regions of the colony, and opened a route to Montreal and to the sea.

Upper Canada was operating as an engineering workshop for trying out ideas on a big scale. The dam at Jones Falls was the largest in North America at the time; the three canal systems — the Rideau, St. Lawrence, and Welland — were the engineering marvels of their day. For steamship owners, it was a time of research and development with a lot of trial and error.

The paddlewheel steamship had many disadvantages, the chief one being a sin in the eyes of the

The walking beam of the Europa *is visible above the paddle box. She had a long, narrow hull that required the installation of supporting arches shortly after she was built.*

shipowner: the lack of cargo space. The engine and boiler took up the most valuable cargo space in the middle of the hull, while cords of wood fuel took up deck space. The paddles increased the width of the ship without a corresponding return in cargo-carrying capacity. One of the reasons the sailing schooner lasted throughout the 19th century was that the masts and sails were above the deck, leaving most of the hull available for cargo. An old-fashioned sailing ship could carry more cargo than a paddlewheel steamship with the same length and beam (width). Only when steamships got larger and more efficient could they fully compete with the sailing vessel. Ship designers, well aware of this problem, found an ingenious solution — the propeller-driven ship, an invention whose use persists into the 21st century.

The first propellers on the Lakes appeared where and when they were most needed, in the Rideau Canal in 1840. With the engine near the stern, the rest of the hull was available for cargo. Just as important was that the hull could be increased in beam to the maximum dimension permitted by the canal locks. Starting in the 1840s, the walking-beam engine was gradually replaced by a new type of steam engine that connected directly to the propeller drive shaft and could use higher steam pressure. Soon, a second cylinder was added to make use of the steam left over from the first cylinder; this process was called *compounding*. And then, near the end of the century, came a third development: the triple expansion engine. The fact that the propeller was placed below the waterline caused some worry that the hull would leak where the drive shaft went through the hull in front of the rudder. After trial and experimentation, the propeller soon became the standard configuration for ships carrying cargo and passengers.

The British had lost a good chunk of North America in 1776, and the War of 1812 turned out to be a draw. There was always the threat of an invasion from the United States. The British were determined to give a boost to colonial trade and colonization and ensure their recovery. To do this, three major projects were undertaken: the construction of the Rideau Canal to bypass the American shore of the St. Lawrence River; improving the St. Lawrence River system of canals and locks to overcome the rapids; and building the Welland Canal to lift ships up more than 300 feet from Lake Ontario to Lake Erie. All these projects made it easier to populate the province, bring in manufactured goods, and develop an export trade across the Atlantic Ocean. As an added benefit, hydraulic power on the Lachine Canal was used to drive factory turbines along the waterway, and this led to Montreal becoming the prime industrial city in Canada. A similar development took place along sections of the Welland Canal.

Early settlers had to cope with what they found in travelling to Upper Canada. Passages across the Atlantic in sailing ships usually took well over a month. Mary Holden's story from 1832 is typical: "We were six weeks getting to Quebec. We did not go ashore there; we landed at Montreal, and we were then towed up the river in Durham boats to Prescott, and then in steam packets to York, and from York, 350 miles, in schooner

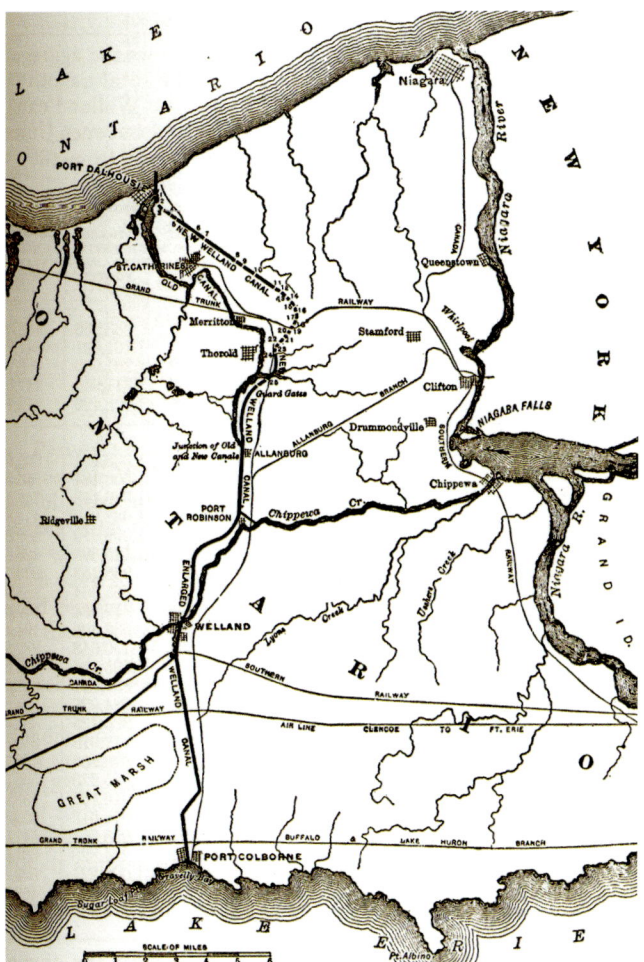

The Welland Canal, first opened in 1829, helped bind Upper Canada politically, and it promoted the expansion of trade by giving access to the Great Lakes bordering the colony.

vessels to Kettle Creek (Port Stanley) and we were then carried in wagons up the country, 66 miles." And then, in the same year there is John Stedman:

> When we got to Prescott we took steam boats to take us to York, 160 miles further still but I in good spirits all the time. I thought we should get there some time, if it was please God. But

Steamboats on the Lakes

Launch of the Great Britain, *Prescott, 1830. Prescott was the easterly terminus of shipping for steamboats and sailing vessels. The St. Lawrence River rapids were a short distance downriver.*

Ontario. In 1826 Colonel John By recommended to Gother Mann, the Inspector-General of Fortifications in England, that the Rideau Canal be constructed as a route suitable for steamboats, all the better to defend Upper Canada. It was a logical decision that acknowledged the rough geography, unsuitable for the towpaths typical of British canals, through the Canadian Shield — and a far-sighted one, since it broke with their canalling experience to date.

when we left Prescott for York, we crossed a lake (Ontario); we was overtaken by a dreadful tempest. We was within 30 or 40 miles of York; we then was driven back on shore, about 80 miles from York again [probably Cobourg].

John and his brother, fed up with the steamboat, walked, thinking they could reach York as soon as the boat. But the steamboat got there first, unloading all passengers, about 250. The route, particularly in the summer, was efficient. A group of immigrants left Prescott on June 29, 1833, aboard the steamer *United Kingdom* for Kingston, where they changed to the Great Britain. By July 1, they were in Toronto. A schooner, the *Trafalgar*, took them through the Welland Canal.

The Rideau Canal was completed in 1832, joining Ottawa to Kingston so ships could move from Montreal, up the Ottawa River, and then to Lake

The objective was to provide a safer way to move military supplies from Montreal to Kingston, to avoid the section of the St. Lawrence River that was subject to attack from the Americans. Despite its origins in the military defence of Canada, the Rideau Canal quickly became a commercial success, as it opened up possibilities for reaching Upper Canada other than the difficult route up the St. Lawrence River. One group of immigrants who benefitted from the opening of the Rideau Canal left England in mid-April of 1834 and arrived near Quebec City on May 23. After clearing the health inspection at Grosse Isle, they were towed by the steamboat *St. George* up the St. Lawrence River to Montreal. They spent the night of June 5 in a warehouse and two days later were on the Ottawa River where, without horses, they had to drag their barge through the Carillon Canal. At Bytown (Ottawa), they were taken in tow by the steamboat *Toronto* headed for Kingston, where they transferred to the *Cobourg* for the passage on Lake Ontario to Toronto. By mid-July they were settled into log cabins built for them at Woodstock. This group were among the very fortunate in that they arrived at their new home quickly and safely.

The Chantler family were among the many unfortunates to arrive in 1832. After crossing the Atlantic they were forced to stop at Coteau-du-Lac waiting for a steamboat. An uncle was sick and so the family was rejected by the local residents.

[We were] obliged at last to go out on the Wharf and get on the underside of the storehouse. We then took the Bed and laid Uncle on it who was quite insensible. I then covered him over with what boards I could find so as to keep the wet off. Uncle continued to get worse and to complete our distress came the rain. As soon as his death was known a coffin was made and his remains were interred in the ground about 3 miles from Coteau-du-Lac. Neither of us followed the coffin to the Grave.

A few days later a Chantler's daughter "grew considerably worse. About 11 o'clock her arms and legs turned Black and her breath was short. Father returned at one o'clock just in time. She was very quiet during the last ten minutes and departed with a sweet smile. Father buried her at the waterside and raised a heap of stones over her."

The year the Rideau Canal opened was the year of the cholera. The first cases were reported at Montreal in early June and at the west end of Lake Ontario later in the month. More than 20,000 immigrants crowded the docks at York, living in damp, unsanitary temporary quarters next to a harbour filled with raw sewage. The new arrivals far outnumbered the local population of 5,000. There is no doubt that the efficiency of the steamboats aided the spread of the disease. Lieutenant-Governor Sir John Colborne acted quickly and dispersed the new arrivals to the western parts of the province as soon as possible, paying the cost of doing so for those who were too poor to afford the fares. Neither Colborne nor the doctors understood how the cholera was spread, but his instincts were right in moving people away from crowded, unsanitary conditions to healthier parts of the province.

The most important of the three canal projects was the ongoing improvements to the system of locks and canals that ran between Montreal and Prescott. The river rapids were the strongest barrier to populating the province and to developing an export trade. This section of the St. Lawrence was overcome using a mix of steamboats, barges, and walking, and was full of terror for many immigrants. They made their way upriver against the rapids in bateaux and Durham boats, and it could easily take twelve days. The boats were poled and pulled upstream by the crew and, when they were fortunate, by a local farmer's ox team. Immigrants often spent the nights in the open with little protection from swarms of insects and rain.

Colonists wanted to avoid the dangerous, labour-intensive, expensive route the British defenders had used during the War of 1812 to strengthen their Great Lakes military bases. A cannon in those years cost more than £600 to transport up the river: it cost £30,000 to move a ship, built in England and sent to Upper Canada in frame like a kit, between Montreal and Kingston. The first section improved to a commercial standard in the mid-1820s was the Lachine Canal, built through Montreal toward Lake St. Louis. The factories using water power along this canal

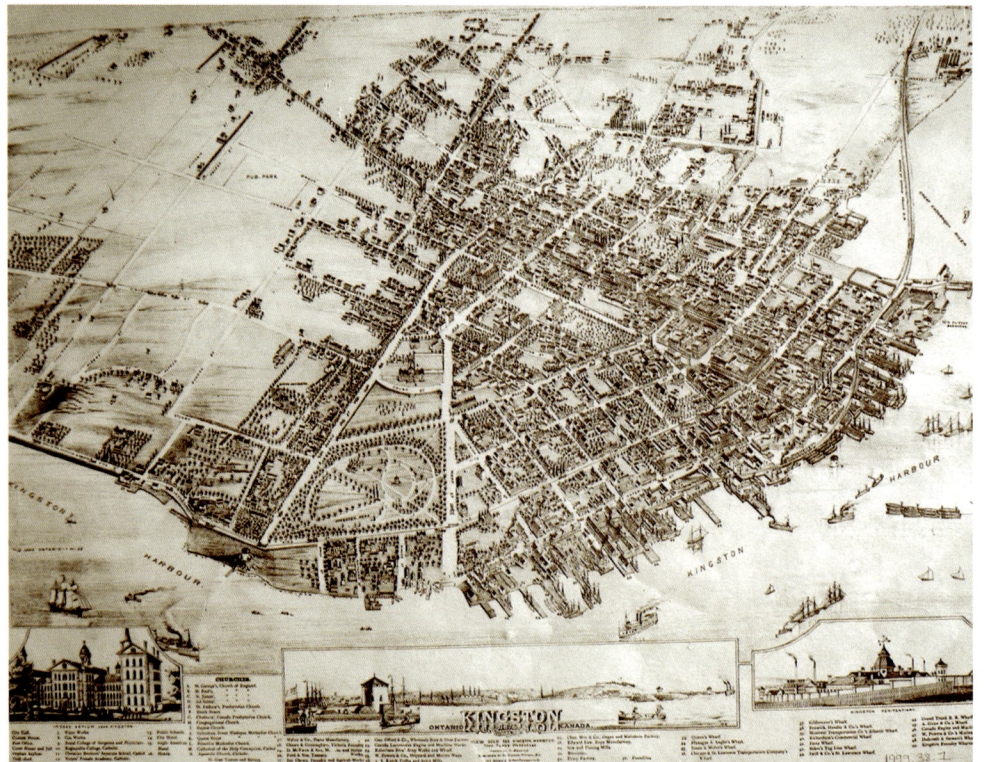
Bird's Eye View of Kingston, 1875. Kingston achieved early prominence as a forwarding port by the 1830s

would soon become the model of industrialization in Canada. Other canals and locks followed along the St. Lawrence River, bypassing rapids, so that by 1848 a ship could sail through to Lake Ontario at a considerably reduced cost in time and money. Given the immensity of the project and the difficulty in getting money, twenty-three years to complete the system was a remarkable achievement.

The "great cataract," Niagara Falls, separated Lake Ontario from Lake Erie and the rest of the province by 326 feet of falling water. The Welland Canal joined Lake Ontario to Lake Erie in 1829. It was positioned as far from the American border as possible for military reasons, as it opened a strategic water route from Lake Huron and Georgian Bay to the Atlantic Ocean. The Welland Canal was the brainchild of private investors and boosters, such as William Hamilton Merritt in St. Catharines, but it was not long before the government had to step in to help finish the job, eventually nationalizing the canal. Lack of money and planning meant that at first the route was all wrong. The first route ran from Port Dalhousie on Lake Ontario to Chippewa, five miles downstream from the Lake Erie end of the Niagara River. Blocks of ice in the early spring, a strong current, and prevailing wind from the west made passages difficult from the new port to the mouth of the Niagara River. By 1833 the engineers had pushed the canal, with forty wood locks, from Port Dalhousie through to Port Colborne, a harbour created as the canal outlet into Lake Erie.

Lake Erie shows its pleasant face to the south. A border runs down the centre, splitting the lake between Canada and the United States, but the south shore has all the advantages, the natural harbours and rivers that evolved into settlements such as Buffalo, Erie, and Cleveland. The arrival of the Erie Canal at Buffalo increased the flow of traffic west to other American ports, making the canal instantly successful and leading to an economic boom and harbour

Canals and the Southern Great Lakes

The formidable height of Niagara Falls had to be overcome by the builders of the Welland Canal.

improvements. The Americans were quick to set up regular shipping lines running from Buffalo to Detroit, starting with their first steamship, the *Walk-in-the-Water* launched in 1818. By the mid-1830s, the U.S. had well over thirty steamboats on the lake.

The north shore, the Canadian shore, is to be avoided. There are harbours — Port Dover and Kettle Creek (Port Stanley) are the most important — but even these are exposed to the prevailing onshore southwesterly winds. Lake Erie is well-named; it has the eerie aspect of a Stephen King novel. Such a large body of water ought not to be so shallow in depth. The mood of the lake is uncertain; you can never be sure what is about to happen. The Canadian north shore is also the killer shore, still known as the great graveyard of ships. Point Pelee and Long Point project into the lake but, when the wind blows strong out of the west, these points disappear into the mist. In the 19th century, early low-illumination lighthouses were unreliable. Magnetic compasses were still primitive and subject to little-understood errors. Steamships and schooners, overcome by winds and heaving seas, ran up on the sandy shores of these points every season. The commercial fishermen are the only real masters of Lake Erie, though they might deny it.

Adelaide, the first Canadian steamboat on Lake Erie, was built at Chippawa in 1833 and was powered with the third-hand Boulton and Watt engine first used in the *Frontenac* (1817). The *Adelaide* was not very successful. American steamboat lines had captured most of the immigrant trade, so *Adelaide* spent most of her time servicing low-traffic, north-shore harbours on Lake Erie, and making runs between Port Colborne and Amherstburg at the Lake Erie end of the Detroit River. The 80-foot Canadian steamship *Lady Colborne* sailed Lake Erie until she was burned by invading Americans during the Upper Canada Rebellion in 1838.

All through the 1830s and beyond, agents in England and Scotland actively recruited immigrants. They found willing passengers, eager to escape the disruptions in their lives caused by the industrial revolution and a class system that kept a large part of their lives in "knuckle to the brow" servitude and limitless poverty. Middle-class families saw opportunities in Upper Canada beyond what they could achieve in Britain. The options open to them included extensive land holdings and jobs in manufacturing and the professions. The great Irish starvation immigration starting in the mid-1840s added to the number of people who saw salvation in British North America. The desperate, the poor, and the ambitious — all were eager to populate Upper Canada, but getting them into the province was dangerous and often deadly. In a remarkably short twenty-five years, private enterprise and mostly government, public works programs created a new transportation system that broke down the natural physical barriers that had separated the colony from itself and the world, a system in which steamboats and steam technology worked best.

4
THE UPPER GREAT LAKES

Sault Ste. Marie was established where the St. Mary River, flowing from Lake Superior to Lake Huron, turns into a run of rapids. When the fur trade declined, the place languished until the Americans built a private canal in 1853, taken over by the state of Michigan in 1855, to accommodate the passage of ships carrying copper and iron ore from Lake Superior south to American foundries and mills. When the Red River Rebellion, led by Louis Riel, broke out in 1869, Canadian troops and supplies were moved by ship from Collingwood to the Soo. In early May 1870, the *Manitoba* managed to get through the American canal carrying supplies to Lake Superior, but the state of Michigan, which owned the canal and was unsympathetic to the British, refused transit of the Canadian-owned *Chicora*. The British who represented Canada in Washington expressed their displeasure and suggested perhaps the Welland Canal might not be open to American ships.

A compromise was reached. Canadian chartered ships unloaded, went through the canal empty, and then recovered military cargo, which had been laboriously moved over a twelve-mile portage road, on the Lake Superior side. There was a steady stream of supplies through Lake Superior to Prince Arthur's Landing (now Thunder Bay) through 1870.

The Assiniboia, *1907. Postcards are works of art, cultural artifacts, and an important source of information for historians.*

Steamboats on the Lakes

Bird's-eye view of Collingwood, which developed quickly as steamship port once a rail link was established with Toronto in 1857.

Dawson's Road, named after the civil engineer who laid it out, was cut to the new province of Manitoba, and the Rebellion came to an end.

The newly formed Dominion of Canada was a minefield of secular and religious differences between the English and French, the Protestants and Catholics, the Irish and British, and Canada and the U.S. The new technology, steamships and trains, served the interests of the Canadian government. In 1885, Louis Riel led another rebellion, but this time the newly built steam railway played the leading role in moving troops to the west.

In 1885 the Canadian government started building a canal of their own at the Soo. The memory of how the Americans treated the Canadian military in 1870 was part of the motivation, but more important was the economic factor: the wealth of the west was being extracted. A canal was needed to move grain, timber, and other bulk goods more efficiently to the south. When the canal, then with the largest lock in the world, opened in 1895, it completed the all-Canadian route from the head of Lake Superior to the Atlantic Ocean. The first ship through was the *Majestic*, built in 1885 at Collingwood for the Great Northern Transit Company. She was trim-looking and of a design that was emulated for many years into the following century.

The symbiotic relationship between ships and trains was particularly intimate in Northern Canada. The railways opened up the north to settlement and the movement of freight. Ships moved grain east from Thunder Bay through the Great Lakes, but only after trains had transported it overland from the prairies in western Canada to the Lakehead. Iron ore rolled down the Algoma Rail tracks to Michipicoten Harbour where it was dumped into the holds of ships for transport to the steel mills to the east. This pattern was repeated with pulpwood and lumber. But always, there was a boom–bust cycle influenced by the changing demand for natural resources in North America and in Europe. Survey parties spread across the north looking for timber, minerals, farmland, and transportation routes.

And the trains pushed relentlessly north. The port of Collingwood had a near monopoly on the passage of freight by ship for about a decade after the rail line arrived from Toronto in 1857. Steamships extended the connections north and west: Chicago had an insatiable need for lumber and sent agricultural goods back east; small settlements along the remote shores of Georgian Bay and into Lake Superior depended on the steamer to bring manufactured goods and essential supplies from Toronto. Surviving a winter in northern communities was more certain when the last of the shipping-season life-line runs arrived before the freezing of the harbours cut off supplies until spring. Collingwood's rail connection made it a natural transfer point for passages to Sault Ste. Marie and into Lake Superior on ships like the *Racine* and the *Chicora* (which was blocked by the Americans in 1870 but

The Upper Great Lakes

A modern artist's rendering of the loss of Waubuno *on Georgian Bay in 1879. The time since the tragedy has diluted none of the effectiveness in portraying another victim of the gales of November.*

carried the Governor-General, Lord Dufferin, on a tour north in 1873). The 137-foot *Asia* was typical of the small, passenger-freight vessels that made regular runs between Collingwood, Owen Sound, and parts north of Manitoulin Island. Dunkan Tinkiss and Christy Anne Morrison, two seventeen-year-olds, survived her loss in Georgian Bay in 1882. She was carrying sixty passengers more than allowed; top-heavy, she went down in mid-September. Tinkiss and Morrison said each time the lifeboat rolled, fewer people were left, until they were the only ones who survived. The bodies slowly drifted ashore.

The *Ploughboy*, another regular visitor to Collingwood, played a small but crucial role in Canadian history. In 1859 her steam engine failed and she started drifting onto the boulders lining the shore of Lonely Island. Among the passengers were the Speaker of the House, Henry Smith, and John A. Macdonald, who must have wondered, "Will your anchor hold when the breakers roar and the reef is near?" The anchor dragged but then held, and a passing steamship rescued the passengers — among them the man who would go on to found the Dominion of Canada, known to Canadians as Sir John A.

Passengers on the *Waubuno* were not so fortunate. The night before the ship's departure, one of the passengers is said to have predicted the ship would be swallowed up. It was not an unreasonable prediction, even in 1879. Georgian Bay was a dangerous place, especially in the season of the gales of November. With lines cast off, the *Waubuno* slipped into Georgian Bay in the snow on the twenty-second day of that treacherous month. She disappeared, with seventy souls.

The navigation tools available to sailors aboard passenger- and cargo-carrying steamships were simple, at least until the mid-20th century when radar was introduced. A typical canal-sized steamship of the 19th century carried charts, a log line, a compass, a barometer, and a wire depth sounder. The traditional "lead, log, and lookout" had been used for thousands of years. The lead line was still used to take soundings by hand to determine the depth of the water. In the 19th century the log was a line towed astern that rotated a dial on the stern rail of the ship, showing the distance travelled — not a particularly good instrument for coastal work, where obstructions and shallow water could snag the rotator at the end of the line. The lookout was just that, an eye on what was going on around the ship, including wind changes in relation to cloud types and the speed of clouds moving across the sky. Rules based on changes in barometric pressure and wind direction helped predict the weather. The weather and its close observation was a constant in the life of a mariner, whether under sail or steam. A sextant might be used to take angles between known points on shore to determine a position on a chart, but it had few other uses on the Lakes. Astronomical navigation was not accurate enough for use on the Great Lakes.

Binoculars typical of those used in the latter part of the 19th century as a navigation aid.

The magnetic compass was by far the most important of the instruments, but even it was subject to error. Some errors were caused by the magnetic influence of metal parts in the ship that deviated the compass from magnetic north. Another error, called variation, common throughout the world, pulled the magnetic-north–seeking needle east or west depending on where the ship was geographically located. If the value of these errors was not known, the compass could not be entirely trusted, and it wasn't until well into the 19th century that these errors were fully identified and correctable. Most vessels made successful passages, especially if the captain was willing to wait out the weather or exercise caution approaching a shore. But then there was ever the "dark and stormy night." The geography of Georgian Bay, Lake Huron, and Lake Superior was especially dangerous when ships had only primitive navigation tools; for example, the confusing and dangerous rock-strewn run into Parry Sound on the east side of Georgian Bay was easy to miss, as were many other ports.

Owen Sound was a rough and ready place full of booze, wild women, and lumbermen. The railway arrived in 1873, and eleven years later Canadian Pacific bought the rail line. The CPR turned Owen Sound into a base for their fleet — and a place of new-found respectability. Wild fun was exchanged for wealth. Canadian Pacific built a legendary fleet of ships with geographical names that honour western Canada. The *Algoma, Athabasca, Alberta, Keewatin,* and *Assiniboia,* with rail connections to the south, carried passengers and freight into Lake Superior. The CPR built the first steel ship in Canada, an important technical achievement. The *Manitoba* was launched at Owen Sound in 1889 to replace the *Algoma,* which went down in a snowstorm on Lake Superior. This new ship was over 300 feet long, used the *Algoma*'s engines, and carried more than 300 passengers. In 1922, a return fare between Owen Sound and Port McNichol cost twelve dollars, meals and berth included; it was an extra five dollars for an automobile. In Owen Sound, CPR built grain elevators that eventually held more than 800,000 bushels of wheat, making the town a link in the vast corporate empire that spread through Canada and across the Atlantic and Pacific oceans.

On December 11, 1911, the Owen Sound connection went bust. The grain elevators burned down. CPR moved across Georgian Bay, giving Port McNichol tem-

Assiniboia at Owen Sound, 1907, part of the Canadian Pacific fleet that made regular runs to Lake Superior.

porary status as a boom town. Parry Sound, Midland, and Depot Harbour also shared in the quick rise and decline of the boom-and-bust phenomenon, which was primarily based on the extraction of resources and the movement of goods between modes of transportation. Most of these communities survive, and some thrive.

The north has always attracted the oversized figures, a mortal match for the huge resources to be cut down or pulled out of the ground and moved in large quantities by steamship. Francis Clergue was a bold Yankee from the state of Maine who taught school and was a law clerk. He built a railway with ordinary tracks and cogs, established a paper mill, and embarked on a dozen other business ventures that mostly failed. His irrepressible energy and ability to charm money from hard-headed investors did not fail him when he arrived at the Soo in 1894. He acquired

The Algoma *went down in 1885 on that inhospitable graveyard of ships, Isle Royale on Lake Superior.*

a municipal, hydro generating plant in return for taking on the debt, thinking that with the combination of electricity and his charisma he would attract business. When that did not happen, he built his own business, a pulpwood plant to use the electricity, followed by ventures in metals, and railways and ships.

Clergue believed in research and development. In 1902, his steelworks started up using the Bessemer process, producing liquid steel to be cast into ingots and rolled into rails for the railway expansion. When a process to improve paper making was discovered by his in-house team, he negotiated with a mining company for the sulphide he needed. He was a man with the right instincts whose hubris was the inability to even consider limits to success. His dictum, that "every part of each product must be used so that no resource could be wasted," sounds surprisingly 21st century. By 1903, the Consolidated Lake Superior Company could not pay its workforce of thousands, so workers rioted in the streets while investors in boardrooms met, schemed, and competed against one another. Clergue was eventually voted off the board in 1907, his power gone. But his accomplishments live on in Algoma Central Railway, Algoma Steel, the Great Lakes Power Company, and the Algoma Central Corporation, which has become a major force in shipping with a fleet of twenty-five ships.

The twin towns and harbours of Fort William and Port Arthur, now merged into Thunder Bay, are the creation of the fur trade, two military expeditions, and the railway. The harbours, strategically located at the head of the Great Lakes, started modestly as a transfer point for furs being moved east. Canadian Pacific completed the first line from Fort William to the west in 1883, and with that the first grain arrived. Ten thousand bushels of wheat were shovelled by hand into wheelbarrows and then dumped into the hold of the *Erin*, a 142-foot steamship built at St. Catharines. A year later a grain elevator was constructed, and a year after that both towns had elevators with a capacity of 1,500,000 bushels. The harbour developed into one of the largest ports in the world for forwarding grain. The competition for grain was so great that two other rail lines followed to transport it. Just prior to World War I, the elevator capacity had increased to 21 million bushels. In one year near the end of the 1920s there were 3,000 ship entries.

As the trade expanded, the ships increased in size. Port Arthur Shipyards was established in 1909 to build steel ships and make repairs. A little over a decade later, they were building 600-foot ships.

In 1868, silver was discovered close to Thunder Cape on a small island, really just a lump of rock, soon to be called Silver Islet. A steamship link with Collingwood was established and the discovery soon attracted international attention. By 1884, when the mine ceased operation, well over $3 million in ore had been extracted. The 1,230-foot mine shaft was considered a great engineering accomplishment. The discovery at Silver Islet led to extensive prospecting around the shores of Lake Superior. The wealth of wood products found in the area turned out to be more valuable than minerals. The first industry to benefit was the railway tie industry that supplied the CPR railway under construction north of Lake Superior. When the railway was completed, the tie industry declined, to be replaced by the pulp and paper industry, largely based in Port Arthur and Fort William. These two towns were the gateway to the west, with steamships providing the most valuable links to the east. Steam technology opened the north — lay the railway tracks and people will come; build the steamships and millions of tons of wood, metals, and grain will be carried to the south.

This grain shovel is made of wood; a metal shovel might produce a spark, igniting precious cargo.

Imagine yourself aboard ship travelling from Collingwood at the south of Georgian Bay to Killarney, then west along the North Channel between Manitoulin Island and the mainland, climbing the gradient of the St. Mary's River, moving through the locks at Sault Ste. Marie into an inland sea, Lake Superior. You have made an instant passage through some of the most spectacular places on Earth. Here are horizons without limit, remote shorelines, steep cliffs, and thousands of islands. Here are difficult channels that still challenge the best wind- and steam-driven ships, even those equipped with official government sailing directions.

Steamboats on the Lakes

The Cambria, *built in 1877, served the railway construction industry during the 1880s on Lake Superior.*

There is a place called "up north" that is a part of the Canadian psyche. It is in the imagination, and it is real. The channel between the world's largest freshwater island, Manitoulin, and the mainland easily qualifies as ideal for connoisseurs of such places. For about eight ice-free months a year, small towns and villages along the North Channel route were dependent on a fleet of small steamboats that carried passengers and freight. It was not until the early 1960s that trucks, fully replacing steamboats, provided twelve months of service.

In 1946, ten dollars would buy two nights' accommodation and five meals aboard the 178-foot SS *Manitoulin*. She made regular runs from Owen Sound on Georgian Bay to Saulte Ste. Marie by way of the North Channel. Among her ports of call were the twelve "Turkey Trail" ports: Killarney, Manitowaning, Little Current, Kagawong, Gore Bay, Meldrum Bay, Blind River, Cockburn Island, Thessalon, Bruce Mines, and Hilton Beach and Richards Landing on St. Joseph Island. For thirty-five dollars, passengers received five nights' accommodation and fourteen meals for a cruise that was advertised as "Different, Delightful and So Inexpensive."

During a summer break from studies at Queen's University, young Gordon Shaw worked as a waiter aboard the SS *Manitoulin*. He described the meals as "of good Ontario quality":

> Breakfast consisted of juices and cereals and, to most, cheese or jam omelets. Luncheons and

The Upper Great Lakes

dinners were both three-course meals starting with soup or juice, then a main course of at least one roast, local fish, or cold cuts, to be finished with a choice of about four types of freshly baked pies. Friday dinners featured baked "North Channel trout" and "Roast Manitoulin Tom Turkey." There were white tablecloths, well-polished silver, and flowers on each table in an elegant wood-panelled dining room. This good food was served without alcohol; the ship was not licensed. This fact did not seem important; many of the passengers enjoyed the beverage of their choice in their rooms.

There were 54 staterooms for 108 passengers, all located on the second or cabin deck, as were small lounges at both the forward and aft ends. These staterooms were basic and about the size of a railway bedroom, with upper and lower berths, a washbasin surmounted by an oval mirror, two lifebelts, and several wall pegs. The toilet and shower facilities were amidships by the funnel, "Gents" to starboard, "Ladies" to port. Four parlour rooms were equipped with a double bed, a washbasin, and a toilet.

We six waiters had lots of laughs. We slept in the "flick," a pie-shaped room in the forward hold shared with the pantryman, two porters, and two dishwashers. Aft of us were rooms for the two oilers, the two firemen, and the four deckhands. Only one small ship's ladder led to the deck above.

The *Manitoulin* carried a crew of about thirty-five: seven officers; eight deck ratings that included wheelsmen, watchmen and deck hands; four engineering ratings, two firemen and two oilers; six waiters, two porters, a pantryman, a tuck-shop attendant, two dishwashers and four cooks. The stowing of freight created a challenge for our first mate. It was diverse in nature, although mostly canned goods, sacks of flour and sugar, and furniture. Loaded in Owen Sound, it had to be stowed in approximately port order to facilitate ready unloading in various ports along the way. Wages were in proportion to fares; deckhands earned fifty-five dollars a month while we waiters earned only forty dollars.

A ladder was needed to reach the upper berth.

The *Manitoulin* was not as luxurious or as big as the crème de la crème of Lakes travel, such as the *Hamonic* or *Keewatin*, but she was more typical of the many steamships that have played a role in the development of the province since 1817 — linking communities, delivering freight, carrying passengers and commercial travellers. *Manitoulin* sailed at the end of an era; there was deference to authority, jackets and ties were commonly worn, and many passengers and crew attended church. Most of the province was made up of small villages and towns linked by the railway, poor roads, and steamships. The *Noronic* fire of 1949 and the post-war boom would change everything.

5

Muskoka

The great rivers and lake routes used by the aboriginal peoples, followed by explorers and fur traders, evolved into the first steamboat routes. Between Montreal and Prescott lay a series of rapids separated by smooth sections that were among the first to see steamboats in Upper Canada. This pattern of "steam on smooth water" was repeated on rivers and lakes throughout Ontario. Engineers connected the water route between Kingston and Ottawa; steamboats on the Ottawa River sailed north; ships plied the old fur trade route between Georgian Bay through Lake Nipissing on to Montreal. Steamboats steadily made their way to the settlement centre of the province on the Muskoka Lakes.

The inland waters of Ontario saw their first steamboats in the 1880s on Lakes Temiskaming and Nipissing. The timber and lumber trade, followed by mining, attracted settlement. Many communities had to wait until the early 20th century for a northern Ontario rail line, and good roads did not appear until after World War II and the development of cottage country. Steamboats, then, provided the essential transportation links. Some of these steamships were small fry in the range of 50 feet, but of importance well beyond their size to those who worked and lived in isolated waterfront communities. There were tugs

Sophisticated in design, this brochure for the Muskoka Lakes uses many of the elements that still attract tourists.

towing log booms, and a few "alligators," a kind of amphibious steamboat able to cross short stretches of land between lakes. The *Inter-Ocean* was the first steamship on Lake Nipissing in 1881, under the ownership of the Muskoka and Nipissing Navigation Company, while the *Mattawan* was the first to appear on Lake Timiskaming in 1882. As everywhere in the province, the railways and changing circumstances in trade turned steamship ownership into a gamble.

So strong was the desire to move cargo by ship across the northern part of the province to the Atlantic Ocean that survey parties were sent out in the 1860s to establish a route from Georgian Bay up the French River into Lake Nipissing, and then via the Montreal River to the Ottawa River flowing to Montreal. Down the St. Lawrence River there was access to the world. The idea died when many saw a railway link as being more useful while, further to the south, the competing Welland and St. Lawrence River canals were in full operation. By the beginning of the 20th century, the north had an abundance of coal, iron ore, grain, copper, nickel, and lumber, mostly moved by ship. In 1909 a full-fledged and well–thought-out Georgian Bay Ship Canal was surveyed so that 600-foot ships could follow essentially the same route as planned in the 1860s. The canal was almost on. Liberal Prime Minister Sir Wilfrid Laurier promised to build the canal if re-elected in 1911. He was not, and the canal moved backstage when a more pressing concern, the prospect of war, appeared on the horizon. The canal was a bold plan that became less practicable as the railway system pressed into northern Ontario.

The government decided to colonize the Muskokas in 1858. Those who first settled the easily accessible regions immediately north of Lake Ontario and Erie were the colonists. Those who arrived in Canada West (as Upper Canada had been called since 1841) later in the century saw an opportunity, took what land was left, or were simply enticed further north into the bush and rock; they are better seen as pioneer settlers. The country was rough and the soil much thinner than the promises of rich farmland. By 1866 the Muskoka Road

The alligator tug towed log booms and could cross short stretches of land between lakes when needed.

was paved with logs, and in the same year the first steamboat on Lake Muskoka, the *Wenona*, was launched. Loggers had been in the area for years, cutting timber that was sent down the lower Muskoka River to Georgian Bay, until the best of the timber on the west side of the lake was gone, most of it to Chicago. The appearance of the *Wenona* solved several problems. She performed the important task of getting settlers and business enterprises into the region. For them she was a passenger and freight boat. To the loggers she was a tug, put to work moving log booms from places like Bracebridge west across the lake to Bala, where they were sent down river to Georgian Bay. It was not long before vast tracts of timber on the east side of Lake Muskoka disappeared, in part with the assistance of the *Wenona* and vessels like her.

The *Wenona* was the first of a fleet owned by the Muskoka Lakes Navigation Company under the leadership of Alexander Peter Cockburn. The planking for her hull was hand-sawn with a whip-saw, leaving

Steamboats on the Lakes

Steamboats at Port Carling, Muskoka Lakes. A busy meeting place for cottagers, and the place where upbound and downbound steamships meet.

along with a canal further north at Port Sandfield, named after the provincial Premier. With the string of lakes joined, the immediate reaction was to cut down all the largest trees that remained. Many of these were exported by a water route from the Muskoka Lakes to Georgian Bay, down the Great Lakes to Quebec City and then across the Atlantic to British markets.

The railway, reaching Gravenhurst in 1875, provided a route for getting lumber to the southern markets and for bringing passengers into the Muskoka Lakes. By 1885, when the *Wenonah* was abandoned, the thin soil of Muskoka had forced many of the settlers off the land, but there were other occupations: working in the bush, labouring at the lumber mill, and providing services for a new industry — tourism. Cockburn's tireless promotion of Muskoka paid off by helping to develop that new industry. A well-developed route was offered by Richelieu & Ontario Navigation Company in the early years of the 20th century. A traveller could board one of their steamships bound to Toronto from Montreal, then catch a Grand Trunk train to Muskoka Wharf, and finally transfer to a Muskoka Navigation Company steamship that delivered passengers in style to the Royal Muskoka Hotel — all for $21.55, with meals and berths extra on R & ON Co.'s steamers.

slivers and lack of fine finish. But she appears to have been well built, and lasted twenty years. Steamboats in these remote regions were on their own. Hulls might be built on a lakeshore but engines were brought in from the south. There were no machine shops to repair failed engine parts, and there were no charts for navigation, only hard-learned local knowledge. The captain, steam engineers, and crew were full of ingenious solutions for engine breakdowns and freeing grounded ships. A.P. Cockburn himself occasionally took command.

Thirty years old and an elected member of the provincial legislature, Cockburn was the supreme Muskoka Lakes booster. As a politician, Cockburn was expected to "bring home the bacon." He quickly used his influence to persuade the government to build a lock between Lake Muskoka and Lake St. Joseph at Port Carling. The lock opened in 1871,

Once the largest trees of the forested Muskokas

were gone, the smaller trees were cut down. By the 1880s there were almost thirty sawmills in the region, fifteen of them clustered around Gravenhurst, which was nicknamed Sawdust City. Steamships and tugs were kept busy moving log booms to the mills and servicing the small villages and towns with new tourist hotels. Many of these opulent hotels achieved a legendary status. The sound of the steam whistle signalling the arrival of guests at the hotel dock transformed a vacation into something exotic and romantic. The resorts had evocative names. Rosseau House was the first of the "wilderness resorts." Windermere House, opened in 1869 and re-built in 1897 after a fire, cost $1.50 a day in the 1880s. A spelling error turned Cleeve Land into Clevelands House. Prospect House started as a boarding house, but would grow to accommodate 300 guests. For the carriage trade, for those who had "arrived" in society, there was the Royal Muskoka Hotel located on Royal Muskoka Island. Formal apparel was expected, there were dances that attracted the celebrities of the day, and, of course, there was the prospect of a round of golf. Built of wood, the Royal met its fate in a fire in 1952. The Royal's fanciful architectural style is emulated in the new museum built at Gravenhurst.

Cockburn knew the tricks of the trade of promotion. As early as 1872, the Press Association of Canada cruised through the Muskoka Lakes aboard the *Nipissing*, and the free cruise paid off in good publicity. By the early 20th century the Muskoka Lakes were well established as the playground of the wealthy, one of the leading resort areas in North America. Familiar names like Seagram, Rockefeller, and Carnegie — and the attendant old money — ran through Cockburn's beloved Muskoka. Today the resort tradition continues. The Muskoka Lakes attract the rich and famous, movie stars, and the "great and good" from Toronto and parts south in the United States. There are "cottages" along the shoreline larger than most family homes. It is a dream place made real. Some of that reality is devoted to preserving the very best of our Canadian watercraft

Train passengers from Toronto walked across the wharf to a fleet of waiting steamships for quick passage to the many Muskoka resorts and cottages (above). Cabin passkey (right).

Steamboats on the Lakes

The Segwun prior to her restoration. She is like honey that draws aficionados and tourists from every part of the world.

traditions. There are scores of fast, highly polished, mahogany-planked motorboats that maintain the wood-boat–building skills of local craftsmen. But more significant is the silent, coal-fired, passenger-carrying steamboat *Segwun*. The *Segwun* is like honey that draws afficionados and tourists from every part of the world. There are few ships that have participated in their own centennial celebrations: in 1987, on the shores of Gravenhurst, more than 5,000 people, including the Honourable Lincoln Alexander, Lieutenant-Governor of Ontario, showed up to celebrate the *Segwun*'s 100th birthday.

The history of the Muskoka Lakes followed a pattern common to many regions across Canada. Steam technology accelerated the process of European arrival, the extraction of resources, settlement, and decline and recovery. There were remarkable people who operated according to the rules of their time. A.P. Cockburn's fleet grew in size, as did his popularity — and his size. Thinking himself too thin as a young man, he deliberately put on weight to conform to the then-accepted image of the successful tycoon, an ample and successful man of the north. Cockburn died in 1905 but his legacy lives on in the *Segwun*. On June 27, 1981, the *Segwun* resumed service as a passenger ship, and she continues to this day. She is the iconic Canadian object powered by steam and propeller. She is alive and available, thanks to the dedication of her many supporters, to those who want to experience steamboat history directly.

6

1880 to the End of World War I

The launch of the Mathewston *at Port Arthur Shipyard, 1922.*

The golden years of steamships on the Great Lakes started in the last quarter of the 19th century. The channels between the Lakes had been deepened to allow the movement of larger and deeper vessels. The average net tonnage, a measurement of internal carrying capacity, of ships going through the U.S. canal at the Soo was 495 tons in 1880, and increased to more than 2,000 tons by the beginning of World War I. Canals and locks were constantly upgraded while the railways developed a more sophisticated relationship with steamship companies, making easier connections for the movement of passengers and cargo. The important lake ports, Toronto and Hamilton, were in firm command as the industrial centres of Ontario, with Sault Ste. Marie and Thunder Bay in the second rank. Toronto's population grew from 56,000 in 1871 to 181,000 twenty years later, while Hamilton's rapid industrial expansion prompted similar growth.

All the major Lakes ports were magnets for immigrants to Canada, who found work in factories and as labourers and cargo handlers. The steel mills in Hamilton had to be fed with iron ore, limestone, and coal, and ships were the cheapest transport available to supply the materials. Thunder Bay was receiving an increasing flow of wheat from the western prairies,

Loading grain c. 1900. The booming grain trade accounted for the establishment of many 20th-century steamship companies.

to be moved by ship, or by ship and rail, toward Montreal. Canadian Pacific's attempt to monopolize the grain trade was broken in the early years of the 20th century with the construction of competing railway lines to the Lakehead.

The turn of the 20th century was a period of unrestricted industrial capitalism, when the sight of smokestacks along a waterfront signalled success. It was a period of staggering growth. In 1880, 1.3 million tons of cargo moved through the U.S. locks at the Soo; by 1906 the figure was 51 million tons. In the same twenty-six period, passengers went from 25,000 to 63,000.

There was now enough capital for single shipowners and partners to establish corporations that grew to own whole fleets of ships. It was a period of rough industrial capitalism, with big companies — coal and steel, for example — swallowing smaller firms and then, in turn, being eaten by larger sharks. Shipping was a highly competitive business that tended towards acquisitions and monopolies. By the latter years of the 19th century there were many shipping companies still run the old-fashioned way, and most of them did not have long to live before being taken over by large corporate interests. The Richelieu & Ontario Steamship Company started in 1875 as a merger of the Canadian Navigation Company of Ontario and La Compagnie du Richelieu. It acquired the St. Lawrence River Steam Navigation Company in 1886, followed by the Northern Navigation Company in 1911, and the Thousand Island Steamboat Company and Niagara Navigation in 1912. The company was reorganized in 1913 as the Richelieu & Ontario Navigation Company Limited. But the greatest takeover of all, with internal machinations orchestrated by Grant Morden and as dramatic as the plot of an opera, occurred as the Richelieu & Ontario Navigation Company was acquired by Canada Steamship Lines on June 1, 1914. CSL is a 21st century survivor, one of the most successful shipping companies in the world, with an ancestry that goes back to the origins of Canada.

James Playfair, a canny Scot who settled in Midland with his partner, established the Midland Navigation Company in 1901 and rolled it over several times. By 1912 the partnership had two companies: the Great Lakes Transportation Company for big ships, over 250 feet, that could sail only the Upper Lakes; the Glen Line for canallers that could transit the St. Lawrence River canal and lock system to Montreal and the sea. These two fleets were combined into the Great Lakes Navigation Company in 1925, and were sold a year later to the Canada Steamship Lines.

Playfair's Midland Shipyard constructed, among others, the canaller *Glencova*, and the *Gleniffer* and

Gleneagles, all for the Playfair fleet. James Playfair lived big. His two steam yachts, the *Pathfinder* and *Venetia*, were what was expected of a shipping tycoon, elegant conspicuous consumption. The sailing ships *Pathfinder* and *Playfair* from Toronto, used today for youth leadership training and partly established by Playfair philanthropy, pay tribute to his name. Long before the days of outsourcing, Playfair established his company as a vertically integrated firm in an attempt to control all aspects of the business. Certainly, the prime exponent of this ideal in the 19th century was D.D. Calvin & Company, based on Garden Island at Kingston. More than sixty ships were built to service Calvin's main source of revenue, the timber trade. Shipping companies that survive in the 21st century follow the pattern set then in having partnering ownerships of shipyards.

The *Cayuga, Chippewa, and Corona saw regular service between Toronto and Niagara River ports.*

Meanwhile, Canada Steamship Lines continued acquiring fleets. The passenger steamships were magnificent — luxurious and beautiful. The Richelieu & Ontario brought with them the *Toronto*, *Kingston*, *Montreal*, *Rapids King*, *Rapids Queen*, and *Rapids Prince*. One great 20th-century shipbuilder, the late Donald A. Page, described the *Kingston* best, as he knew it from direct experience:

She was built in Toronto by the Bertram Engine Works Company Ltd., was designed by A. Angstrom, who, in turn, was greatly influenced by the work of the Detroit naval architect Frank E. Kirby. The vessel had a beautiful fine-lined hull, surmounted by a wide, sponsoned main deck, carried out to the full width of the paddle wheels. Above it stood the light and spacious three-decked superstructure, which housed the passengers. It was a spectacular display of domes and frescoed ceilings, Corinthian columns, curving staircases and potted palms, well suited to the sophisticated passengers of the day. Excellent meals were served in the splendid, panelled salon. In contrast, the individual passenger cabins were rather austere, with an upper and lower berth, a wash basin and single chair in each one.

In the Niagara Navigation Company was the *Turbinia*, the first turbine-driven ship to cross the Atlantic Ocean from England to North America, as

Steamboats on the Lakes

Mine sweeping trawlers at sea. They were among the first purpose-built ships for the emerging Canadian Navy; many were built at various Great Lakes shipyards during WW1.

well as the other passenger freight ships, the *Macassa, Modjeska, Cayuga,* and *Chippewa*. The *Chippewa,* designed by Frank Kirby, was a low-slung beauty with a sweeping sheer over her 308-foot length. The Northern Navigation Company fleet included the *Noronic, Hamonic,* and *Huronic,* as well as the older *Belleville, Caspian,* and *North King*. Aboard the *Hamonic* in 1936, one satisfied customer reported, "The Northern Navigation Company has expedited things by appointing a charming young hostess — not the sort of chaperone one expects to find, but a sweet young lady, who seems to sense every situation and meet it — whose only duty is to make people acquainted with each other, arrange card parties, and other entertainments, and make things generally pleasant."

It is no wonder that the passenger ships were the attention-getters, but the real money was in transporting grain, coal, and other bulk cargoes. The Merchants Mutual Line brought the *J.H. Plummer* and *A.E. Ames* to the CSL fleet. In 1919, acquisition of the Montreal Transportation Company based at Kingston brought in tugs, barges, and lakers, including the *Stormount* and the *Westmount*. CSL had become a shipping giant.

During World War I, Britain assumed direct responsibility for defending the sea approaches to Canada. Naval planners, with their decided bias towards ocean-based shipyards and shipping, considered the Great Lakes something of a backwater. And yet, the shipyards of this industrial heartland of North America responded to the urgency of war by building and operating increasing tonnages of merchant ships. Great Lakes shipyards constructed the first purpose-built warships for the Canadian Navy, which, established in 1910, had grown

by war's end to 5,000 men engaged in coastal patrol, minesweeping, and anti-submarine work. The TR series of jaunty-looking trawlers were modest at only 125 feet, but what they lacked in size they more than made up for in good sea-keeping qualities. One of these, HMCS *Ypres* (built in Toronto), while serving as a gate vessel in Halifax Harbour to keep out German submarines, was sunk in 1940 by HMS *Revenge*. A larger and altered version of these little ships, the corvette, would be built in World War II by the same Lakes shipyards.

Numerous commercial ships were built for war service to replace heavy losses at sea. All under 250 feet in length, they were small enough to gain access to the sea through the locks on the St. Lawrence canal system. Immediately after World War I, Lakes shipyards embarked on an ambitious program to help construct a fleet of merchant ships for Canada.

Top: The Chippewa. *The walking beam and sidewheels are visible, as is the promise of what every shipowner desires— calm seas and a prosperous voyage.* Bottom: A rare view of the Toronto *under construction. The sponsors are typical of the paddlewheeler in that they extend the deck beyond the sides of the hull to gain passenger and cargo space.*

7

Between the Wars and World War II

Any 1920s waterfront was dominated by king coal. In 1920, one authority claimed that 24 million tons of the stuff was moved on the Lakes in one year. Coal was everywhere, and whoever hung the washing out to dry knew better than to do it when the wind was coming from the direction of the docks. It seemed as if the entire world was powered by steam engines, and their black soot everywhere was a fact of life.

In the early 1920s there were more than 1,000 ships with steam engines and boilers listed for the Great Lakes, almost 25% of them Canadian. The Scotch boiler, with the water heated by the passage of fire through tubes, was the most common. A typical engine was triple expansion, with three cylinders so that excess steam not used in the first high-pressure cylinder was passed on to the other two. The engine had come a long way from what Boulton and Watt used in the *Frontenac*.

The shipping industry experienced a boom period following World War I, but for the shipyards the good times were short-lived. The Canadian government subsidized the construction of the Canadian Government Merchant Marine in the early 1920s, and some of the smaller ships, those in the range of 250 feet, were built on the Great Lakes. The ships

The Northern Navigation Company offered a spectacular range of cruises into the upper Lakes.

Between the Wars and World War II

The record-setting arrival of the LeMoyne *at Kingston, 1932. Larger ships now had access to Lake Ontario from the upper Lakes after the opening of the enlarged capacity of the Welland Canal.*

were christened with names intended to carry the idea of Canada around the world. The *Canadian Farmer*, *Rover*, and *Beaver* are evocative examples of this strategy. The *Canadian Beaver*, built at Kingston, survived into World War II, when she was captured by the Japanese in 1941 and then sunk by the United States Air Force in 1944.

By the mid-1920s, the shipping industry had intimations of bad times ahead. In the miserable 1930s, the worldwide Great Depression sent ships "to the wall," a term used by the shipping industry to describe ships not in service. Companies closed down and survivors put patches on patches when they could little afford repairs to their vessels. Shipbuilding dwindled almost to extinction.

Mr. N. M. Paterson, an outstandingly successful merchant, started in Fort William with one grain elevator in 1912. By 1928 he had well over one hundred elevators, most in Manitoba and Saskatchewan, and his facilities in Fort William had expanded. To complete his grain shipments east he used the services of steamship companies, although not always getting the best deal. So he dabbled in ship ownership, starting with the SS *Van Allen*, and in 1926 he established Paterson Steamships Limited, buying eleven ships and a few years later having eighteen canallers built in England. For the next sixty years the company was a force in the shipping industry, but in 2002, when most of the export grain business had shifted west to the Pacific coast, they pulled out to concentrate on the land-based grain industry of the western provinces. Many of their ships were sold to Canada Steamship Lines.

Economies of scale were demanding that ships grow in size. Any vessel over 250 feet used to be confined to the Upper Lakes, that is, Lake Erie to Lake Superior. To carry cargo to Montreal, ships had to be

The machine shops at Collingwood Shipyards were fully active during World War II after the quiet of the Depression.

small enough to get through two bottlenecks: the Welland Canal and the St. Lawrence River canal system. But in 1932 the Welland Canal jumped in size. Upper Lakes vessels could now get to the grain elevators at Kingston on Lake Ontario and a little beyond, to Prescott on the St. Lawrence River, and this opened up opportunities for the industry.

Gordon Leitch knew the grain trade inside out, and wanted to establish grain elevators in Toronto. To do that successfully, he needed ships that would carry the grain for his company at the best rates. Rival shipping companies with a vested interest in moving grain to Georgian Bay and other ports had ganged up on him. They used their business influence to deprive him of good grain rates. With the backing of investors, including James Playfair from Midland, Leitch built a grain elevator in Toronto in 1928. The stalwart Captain Bruce Angus helped him find the *Sarnian*, a 324-foot ship that had been built in 1895. Sixty-seven thousand dollars later, Leitch had a one-ship firm, the Northland Steamship Company. The Toronto elevator was a success, and so the fleet grew, but Leitch found it necessary to bring in James Norris, the hockey-team owner from Chicago. They formed a difficult partnership, but it worked. And all of this in the midst of the economic depression. The new firm, the Upper Lakes and St. Lawrence Transportation Company Ltd., rapidly built up a mixed fleet that included the *Blue Cross*, *John B. Richards*, and the *Ralph Budd*. An idea that had limited success in the 19th century worked brilliantly for them: they bought Barge *137* and used ships of their fleet to tow it to loading docks and back to their elevator. This "consort" system made them money and their company grew into one of the giants. The *Ralph Budd* led a charmed life. Deemed a constructive loss when she ran up on the Keweenaw Peninsula on Lake Superior in 1928, she was recovered by salvagers J.T. Reid & Sons. They did the job right, operating her until 1938 when they sold her to Upper Lakes Shipping. It was the *Budd* that regularly towed the whaleback Barge *137*.

As always, new ships were needed and old vessels had to be repaired. Major shipyards building in steel were established at Port Arthur, Collingwood, and Kingston just prior to World War I. The yard at Port Arthur was magnificent in its scope, with purpose-built brick buildings full of windows, its own generating plant, and a drydock to take the largest of ships. The Collingwood yard extended the facilities developed in the 19th century and stayed in business until 1986. The Kingston Shipyards leased the drydock that had been built by the federal government in 1890, but closed down in 1968, after struggling for a few years when the newly opened St. Lawrence Seaway, accommodating larger ships, put smaller yards out of business. The drydock is now a National Historic Site, and the historic shipyard buildings have been converted into the Marine Museum of the Great Lakes.

Between the Wars and World War II

Yards opened, partly in response to the World Wars, and then closed. James Playfair's Midland Shipyards opened in 1916, closed in 1929, and then reopened in 1940 for wartime construction. One of their great achievements was the *LeMoyne* in 1926, a 640-footer that established records for carrying grain and coal. The end came in 1955. Their last ship was the *T.R. McLagan,* a cooperative shipbuilding venture with Collingwood Shipyards. She was named after the irascible president of Canada Steamship Lines. At 714 feet, she was initially resisted by the St. Lawrence Seaway officials as too long for the locks, but CSL won that battle to increase the size of ships allowed to go through the locks.

The dredge Primrose, *owned by Canadian Dredge & Dock — among the many specialist vessels needed to build and maintain the St. Lawrence Seaway.*

After World War II, the Muir Drydock closed down at Port Dalhousie, and in 1947 the Port Weller Shipyard was opened above Lock One of the Welland Canal. Since pumps were not needed to fill or empty the dock, it was an ideal place for a drydock. The Port Weller Shipyard is still operating with some equipment acquired from the closed-down Collingwood yard.

There were many smaller yards building barges, tugs, and harbour craft. Among the most distinguished was the Toronto-based Polson Yard; its Owen Sound branch had built the first steel ship in Canada in 1889. The Owen Sound building yard evolved into Russel Brothers, who built alligator vessels for the timber industry and superb small tugs for use in World War II. All the shipyards in Toronto have disappeared, their lands part of a controversial stop–start urban regeneration plan. In the 1930s at Kingston, the 19th-century Davis Drydock site became Canadian Dredge and Dock. They boomed during the construction of the St. Lawrence Seaway, when they built and provided maintenance for the specialist tugs and dredges needed for the construction of locks and canals. The yard is now Metal Craft Marine, whose small 200-foot drydock is among the most valuable repair and inspection facilities at the east end of the Great Lakes.

Being a sailor is not all runs ashore and happy times. Stokers, wipers, and engineers worked in the bowels of the ship. Stokers were a breed unto themselves, working in a small version of hell — the boiler room — with heat, sweat, and coal dust as constant companions. They had a tough reputation that was based on shared work, muscles, and strength. Stoking the fires and shovelling tons of coal required the skill to save money and keep the operating costs down. Wipers were generalists in the engine room, carrying wiper rags in their back pockets to remove excess oil from the engine. It was dangerous work, putting their hands into and around the moving parts of a steam engine. The engineers had charge of the main engines and all the auxiliary engines used to pump boiler water and bilges, to generate electricity, and to operate the deck winches. Although they were subordinate to the captain, they were ultimately in physical control of the ship.

A captain on the bridge would send orders to the engine room with an engine-room telegraph: full ahead, half ahead slow, reverse. The engineer would send the order back to the bridge to show he had read and understood it. Then he turned valves, kept an eye on the gauges, shifted levers — all heavy, oversize gear. The captain had to understand what the engine could do and anticipate the time needed for the engineer to make the engine perform as required, especially when approaching other ships or a dock. The engines had to be reliable. Lake ships worked in open water and passed close to one another in narrow channels. In canals and locks it took great skill to get a ship from any harbour to another without mishap.

The telegraph was used to send orders from the bridge to the engine room.

The sailors were rated as seamen, able seamen, wheelsmen, or bosuns. There were cooks and cook's helpers; maybe a steward. The hours were long. Most of the crew in the early days of cargo-carrying steamships lived in the forward part of the ship, in the forecastle. The crew of passenger ships lived deep and usually well forward in tight spaces; on the SS *Manitoulin*, the small room in the forward hold was called the "flick." Sailors handled lines, removed and replaced hatches, chipped rust from the decks, and painted. They were general labourers in a mobile, industrial setting. Riveted ships always leaked, decks over the sleeping space were constantly covered in water. And there was the funk in the crew's quarters. The air was thick with smoke, the smell of dirty socks and well-used bedding. Sanitary facilities were primitive until after World War II.

Prior to the war, ships took a long time to load and unload cargo; this meant longer runs ashore. Montreal was the favourite stop ashore, rife with taverns and brothels. Many a sailor got left behind, but there were always replacement sailors looking for work, often along the Soulanges Canal. To the north on Lake Superior, in the no man's land between Port Arthur and Fort William, there were houses of pleasure known by sailors everywhere. But not every sailor matched the stereotype of the hard-drinking womanizer. Many of the ports had well-equipped sailors missions that provided good accommodation, a bath, and a place to meet local people. They still exist for sailors.

To landlubbers ashore, sailors were at the bottom

of the social pecking order. The popular film *Mutiny on the Bounty*, released in 1935, along with the Nordoff-Hall books in 1932, set in the public's mind a mixed image of the sailor — fundamentally loyal, loutish, and brave, and at times given to rebellious behaviour, like boys everywhere. This image of the simple sailor, and the paternalism that followed from the shore-bound decision-makers, was essentially negative. Organizing a union for sailors was more difficult than organizing a union for factory workers, with sailors constantly on the move, but their living conditions onboard, the long hours, and minimal pay cried out for redress. Organizers had to buck the traditions of the sea. The old legal culture of the sea, based on long passages aboard sailing ships, had not evolved in step with the working conditions faced by men in steel ships in coastal and Lakes shipping. The attitude in the 1930s from the shipowners and captains was, "Count yourself lucky you have a job — and don't complain!" The captain's word was still the ultimate authority regarding all aspects of a sailor's life aboard ship, and sometimes ashore as well, especially if the sailor was a hometown boy known by the captain.

Out of this miasma emerged the National Seamen's Association, founded by Captain Newbold McMaster.

Sailors had far less protection than factory workers ashore but, as always, they made the best of a situation. There was no help for the sick or injured.

In reality, he was a shipping company man in disguise; in the face of a strike in 1935, when his leadership was needed, he backed down. In stepped a brilliant organizer, Joe Salsberg, who stage-managed a settlement and the establishment of another union — the Maritime Workers Union of the Great Lakes. And then there appeared the unprepossessing Communist Pat Sullivan, founder of the Canadian Seaman's Union and a first-class organizer, who made some gains for the sailors at the end of the 1930s and into the early '40s. At the beginning of the War, Communists were the "bad guys" because the Soviets were in league with Germany, and as a result Pat Sullivan was interned. When Hitler invaded Russia in 1941, almost overnight Stalin became Uncle Joe, and the

Communists, allies. Sullivan was released in 1942. The Canadian Seaman's Union made a no-strike pledge for the rest of the war — putting off an inevitable conflict between shipowners and sailors.

In the mid-1930s, Canada Steamship Lines, owners of the "ocean liners of the Lakes," had positioned themselves to attract American tourists. A 1936 brochure boasted of "The Finest Cruises on the Finest Ships on the Greatest Inland Seas in The World":

> The majestic ships *Noronic* and *Hamonic* are the largest and finest liners on the Great Lakes. The flagship is almost 400 feet long, has six decks, stateroom accommodation for 562 passengers, dining saloon seating 274 passengers on the observation deck, six times around which makes a mile. In service, cuisine, comforts, conveniences and appointments, these ships are not surpassed on inland waters. Staterooms are comfortable and all with running water. Parlors equipped with beds, private bath and toilet are also available.

The first morning of the cruise featured "a beach picnic at Canatara…bathing, dancing — all in a lovely setting…golf at the Sarnia Golf Club followed by dinner and the evening get together." This clever scheduling allowed the ship to go alongside a Canada Steamship Lines dock in Sarnia to take on freight and supplies while in Canadian waters. The route took them through Sault Ste. Marie and into Lake Superior. There was afternoon tea at Port Arthur, golf

In the middle of the Great Depression, steamship companies appealed to Americans from the midwest for business with attractive and elegant brochures.

at the country club, and the "magnificent panoramic views of Duluth, 800 feet above sea level." The ships returned by the same ports. Passing downbound through the Soo, the ship entered the St. Mary River, where calm waters were assured for "the last evening aboard with the major climax of the entire cruise, the Masquerade Ball — exciting, gay, unforgettable — where many new friendships are cemented."

The *Hamonic* and the *Noronic* made regular departures from Detroit on Friday and Monday, arriving back the same day a week later. The cruise package, including coach fare on the train to Detroit from Chicago and a berth in a comfortable inside cabin, was $71.40 return. Upgrade to an outside berth was an additional ten dollars. From Nashville, the same cruise package was eighty dollars return.

The Noronic, *one of the largest and finest liners on the Great Lakes.*

Shipping companies and shipyards barely survived the Depression years of the 1930s. Three firms that survived until well after World War II were Scott Misner Steamships, the Hall Corporation, and Algoma Central Corporation, which celebrated its centennial in 1999. Add Canada Steamship Lines, Paterson, and Upper Great Lakes, and you have the big six.

The yards were poorly prepared for the outbreak of World War II after lean times in the 1930s. There was an immediate need for merchant and naval shipping. The Canadian Navy had only ten fighting ships in 1939; by the end of the war, the fleet had more than 400 ships. Great Lakes shipyards made their contribution to the Canadian, British, and American navies, building fifty-one corvettes, seventy-six Bangor-class minesweepers, and a variety of smaller craft.

Most of these small warships were equipped with reciprocating steam engines that, once started, had to stay in continuous operation for the duration of the long trans-Atlantic passages. Many vessels, their hulls built from the Kingston Shipyards to the Port Arthur Shipyards at Thunder Bay, served under the worst of conditions at sea — winter North Atlantic. The Lakes shipbuilders did the best job possible.

HMCS *Weyburn* was launched at Port Arthur Shipyards in the fall of 1941. On her passage down the Lakes, from near the centre of Canada to the Atlantic Ocean and to the war, she passed through Montreal, where a young man, Wilfrid Bark, may have seen her pass by. A year later, at the age of twenty-one, Bark was in the Canadian Navy, training as

The Masquerade Ball was a passenger-ship tradition — here, aboard the Manitoba *in 1940.*

an officer in Halifax. Young men from across Canada, many new to the sight of any large body of water, willingly joined the Navy. Two months later Bark was aboard *Weyburn*. He wrote home that "you don't realize how dumb you are till you hit the sea, and if people weren't considerate, life could be mighty tough." Across to Scotland aboard the *Weyburn* for more training, Bark was apprehensive about his first encounter with posh-sounding Englishmen at the training base. To him they were all snobs, but eventually his residual memory of Canadians being treated as colonials disappeared — somewhat.

HMCS *Weyburn* was sent to a mysterious destination in the Mediterranean Sea. As the officer responsible for censoring the crew's mail, Bark was aware of the warning, "Loose lips sink ships"; nonetheless he managed to get a letter through to his parents with a broad hint as to his whereabouts: "Think of Prudential Life." His parents were grateful to know he was at Gibraltar. By this time, Bark had a good friendship with Captain Tom Goldby, the ship's Canadian commanding officer. The crew had the best Christmas possible, and on Boxing Day, in another letter to his family, he wrote that "next Christmas when I'm home, we'll be able to compare it with not too much difference."

Bark's ship was sent to the north coast of Africa for Operation Torch. West of Gibraltar the *Weyburn*, moving up to position on the side of the convoy, struck a mine. Confidential papers onboard were quickly disposed of while other ships took off her survivors. Twenty minutes passed quickly and then a bulkhead gave way, the bow lifted up, and the Port Arthur–built *Weyburn* slid into the sea. Nine men were lost, including Sub Lieutenant Wilfrid Bark.

All that remains as a memorial to this young man is a small brown suitcase, the kind carried by officers — inside were letters from home, medals, certificates of appreciation from king and country, and a posthumous Mention in Dispatches. Wilfrid Bark served the Canadian Navy for twelve months; the corvette, from commissioning to loss, fifteen months. In all, thirty-three Canadian naval vessels were lost due to enemy action.

Desperate times during World War II sent ships designed for Lakes service to sea, and the steamship companies had losses, most by shelling and torpedoes: CSL, five; Paterson, eleven; and Upper Lakes, six. Among the ships lost were the *Donald Stewart*, *Portadoc*, and the *Frank B. Baird* — all vintage Lakers — three lonely merchant ships in a great sea, extinguished by torpedoes and gunfire from U-boats. These three plain-looking, 250-foot, team-engined canallers, designed to get the job done on the Great Lakes and nothing more, were finished off in the Strait of Belle Isle between Newfoundland and Labrador; off Sierra Leone, Africa; and southeast of Bermuda, respectively. The submarine that sank the *Donald Stewart* in September 1942, the *U-517*, was seen by HMCS *Weyburn* in the Gulf of St. Lawrence in March 1942. The U-boat, on the surface, had fired two torpedoes at the canaller, *Donald Stewart*. One missed and the other struck her target. The

HMCS Weyburn, *built at Port Arthur Shipyards for the Canadian Navy. She struck a mine and was lost off the north coast of Africa.*

explosion from the *Stewart*, loaded with gasoline on deck, was seen twenty miles away. The *Weyburn*, scheduled to cross the Atlantic Ocean, had only six months to live when it saw the *U-517* in the Gulf of St. Lawrence. Many other Canadian and Newfoundland companies shared in the losses during the conflict; sixty-seven ships and more than 700 merchant ship sailors did not come back.

8

AFTER WORLD WAR II

Alan Howard was one of those larger-than-life characters who woke up zealous each morning and did not stop at night until his dreams were just right. Polio had taken away the use of his legs, so he used a leather seat with four wheels that sat about six inches off the ground. He could shoot himself down the hallway of the old Marine Museum of Upper Canada like a modern-day special Olympian. Going up the worn stone stairs to the upper floors, he used his arms to lift his bottom, step by step. Although his sense of humour was enhanced by his love of Gilbert and Sullivan, his passion was steamboats, and one in particular — the *Cayuga*. In 1953 he was the Managing Director of the Cayuga Steamship Company Limited.

To understand the strength of Howard's passion and conviction, one has to go back a few years to September 17, 1949. More than 500 passengers boarded the *Noronic* at Detroit and Cleveland, with Toronto as a mid-cruise stop on the way to Kingston and the Thousand Islands. By two in the morning most of the passengers were in their cabins, but one late arrival strolling down a corridor noticed smoke at the bottom of a closet door. He ran for help, and soon there was a nineteen-year-old porter standing in the corridor with him, inserting the key. They did their best to extinguish

The Cayuga *made regular sailings from Toronto to the Niagara River after the War, until it could no longer compete with automobile and air travel.*

After World War II

The Noronic *burned in 1949 at the dock in Toronto, with 119 lives lost. This tragedy was the beginning of the end for passenger steamships on the Great Lakes.*

the fire but it grew out of control. Eight or ten minutes later, the alarm was sounded. The firemen poured so much water into the ship that it sank at the dock at Toronto; 119 lives were lost. The owners, Canada Steamship Lines, were censured for failing to take proper precautions and the captain for "fighting the fire as an ordinary seaman" instead of taking command. The official inquiry also said that the fifteen-man skeleton crew aboard was below the safety minimum.

The government stepped in immediately, introducing stricter steamship inspection regulations. They had good reasons, including the unsafe but commonly used flammable oil-based paints that covered wood. Earlier in the same year, the *Northumberland*, fitting out at Port Dalhousie, had burned, but no lives were lost. There were two other fires that stiffened the resolve of the government to take tough action. In 1945 the passenger-freight vessel the *Hamonic* caught fire while alongside the dock at Sarnia, Ontario. The culprit was a gas-operated forklift truck. Captain Horace Beeton backed the ship away from the burning freight shed and beached the *Hamonic*

The charred remains of the Noronic's *dining room.*

alongside a mobile crane. The crane, swinging its bucket back and forth between the ship and shore, carried the passengers and crew to safety like so much freight. The captain's conduct was exemplary.

In 1950, a year after the loss of the *Noronic,* the *Quebec* caught fire in the Saguenay River. The captain took charge, running the ship ashore and alongside a dock, while the mate gathered the passengers on the car deck. One family was lost when they attempted to recover their possessions. Many suspected arson.

The owners' response to the loss of the *Noronic* was immediate. They faced damage claims, and they knew the new regulations would demand extensive refits on old ships. The war years, with their emphasis on strategic shipping, had taken a toll on the maintenance of civilian vessels. Canada Steamship Lines had, to a certain extent, anticipated change by ordering the engines for a new passenger ship, but 1949 and the death of the company's passenger-ship champion, Mr. William H. Coverdale, changed all of that. CSL gave up on the project and started closing down the passenger-ship division. The engines intended for the new ship were used in four bulk carriers — the *Hochelaga, Coverdale, Sir James Dunn,* and *Thunder Bay* — all built at the company shipyards at Midland, Collingwood, and Port Arthur (Thunder Bay). With the loss of the *Noronic,* the carefully constructed network of passenger ships, each on a route complementing the other routes, collapsed. On the Great Lakes, the *Kingston* and the *Rapids Prince* were taken out of company service in 1949, and the *Cayuga* followed shortly after.

Alan Howard was among some 1,200 steamboat enthusiasts who raised the money to buy the *Cayuga* from Canada Steamship Lines for $100,000. The price included the docks at Niagara-on-the-Lake and Queenston. The *Cayuga* was to return to the Toronto–Niagara run she had been designed for when she was built for the Niagara Navigation Company in 1906.

The *Cayuga* went back into service in June 1954,

After World War II

with fares of $3.25 adult return and $1.50 for children. The ship was popular and she easily carried more than a thousand passengers, but there were nagging problems. Among the new shareholders in the ship was D. Roland Michener, Q.C., later to become Governor-General of Canada. It was a dream team of the influential, the great, and the good. But the new owners were operating the ship on a tight budget. Never far away were the government inspectors. Stung themselves by the *Noronic* fire, they were diligent in their demands for changes and new equipment. After three years there were mounting debts. When *Cayuga* made only two of her three scheduled trips on Labour Day 1957, it was the end. In the fall of 1961 she was broken up. Alan Howard, as the curator of the new Marine Museum of Upper Canada, saved artifacts from the ship for the Cayuga Room at the museum.

After World War II, there was a new-found mobility for the average man, similar to the bicycle craze a century earlier, and its most potent expression was found in the sprawling suburbs that sprouted around Ontario's major city, Toronto. More people than ever were sharing in the wealth created by the post-war boom. Don Mills and Scarborough were more than just thousands of new houses. The automobile made suburbs possible. Almost overnight, labourers and the

Top: The entrance hall of the Cayuga. *The palaces and great houses of Europe were a great inspiration to interior designers; they copied that style into opulent surroundings for the passengers. Bottom: It is no wonder the* Cayuga, *seen here in 1928, was the passion of Mr. Alan Howard.*

Steamboats on the Lakes

The steamship Edmonton *a 250-foot canaller. Once numbering in the hundreds and now too small, this type of ship quickly disappeared after the opening of the St. Lawrence Seaway.*

middle class could get out and go where they wanted. The negative effect on the steamboat passenger trade was immediate. In 1965, the *Keewatin* and *Assiniboia*, both owned by Canadian Pacific, joined the parade of passenger ships to be laid up. Even tougher steamboat regulations in the mid-1960s and the competition from automobiles and air travel all contributed to the downfall of the steam-driven passenger ship.

For cargo-carrying steamship companies and shipbuilders there were good times ahead. Port Weller Shipyards was established in 1947 and later acquired by Upper Lakes Shipping, where they had built the *Frank A. Sherman* with a steam turbine engine. Canada Steamship Lines, anticipating the post-war boom, purchased four shipyards located at Thunder Bay, Collingwood, Midland, and Kingston. There were many smaller yards that specialized in building tugs, barges, dredges, and pleasure craft, and doing conversion work.

In the midst of this building boom, the owners had to face up to changes in the industry. Labour and safety laws were getting cleaned up and, after years of little protection for workers, the unions were gaining in strength. There were hundreds of riveted 250-foot canal-sized ships on the Lakes that needed repairs, but the opening of the St. Lawrence Seaway meant these ships were replaced with longer, all-welded vessels. The government, seeing the potential of the Seaway, set up a shipbuilding subsidy that the shipowners called "the angel plan."

After decades of talk with its international partner, the United States, the Canadian government went ahead and built the St. Lawrence Seaway almost entirely alone. It was among the last great infrastructure projects for the shipping industry. A redesign and upgrade to the St. Lawrence River canals project had been begun by the British Government in the 1840s. The Welland Canal, at the west end of Lake Ontario, had been enlarged in 1932, allowing the large ships on the Upper Lakes access to Lake Ontario. The 633-foot *LeMoyne* passed through the Welland Canal in August 1932, carrying 530,000 bushels of wheat. It was a record breaker, but Kingston was as far east as the ship could go. With

After World War II

the opening of the Seaway in 1958, the bottleneck to the sea was broken. Overnight, the size of ships permitted through the locks jumped from 250 feet to 500 or 600, and eventually to over 700 feet. Ships from the middle of the continent had access to the sea, while cities and towns throughout the Lakes could imagine themselves seaports. In the late 1960s the government started a rehabilitation of the Welland Canal, another engineering project that

Top: The Simcoe, *a small bulk carrier, was the first commercial ship to pass through the canals at the opening of the St. Lawrence Seaway in 1959. Bottom:* John S. Pillsbury, *1940. The 250-foot canallers survived the enlargement of the Welland Canal in 1932, but quickly disappeared after the opening of the Seaway in 1959. Many harbours were also enlarged at this time.*

Steamboats on the Lakes

These 21st-century sailors aboard the bulk carrier, Rt. Hon. Paul J. Martin, *live in a demanding environment that requires professionalism and the ability to work together. They are a direct link to an earlier time of life afloat.*

attracted international attention. Many harbours throughout the Lakes were enlarged around this time.

Labour unrest had been put on hold during World War II. Sailors worked a twelve-hour day, seven days a week. When the war ended, the Canadian Seaman's Union (CSU) demanded an eight-hour day and other benefits. Most of the shipping companies, through the Shipping Federation of Canada, had signed on with the Seafarers International Union (SIU). The president of the CSU called for support from other unions, resulting in a twenty-eight–day strike that reached across the Atlantic to the docks of Britain, and resulted in a loss of 45,000 working days.

Prime Minister Winston Churchill, England's wartime leader, delivered his Iron Curtain speech in March 1946. Stalin received faint praise, but there was no doubt Churchill was issuing a warning that the former Soviet friend whose forces had lost more lives than the Western allies combined was now the Communist enemy. Witch hunts for "Commies" took place in the United States and, to a lesser extent, in Canada. Innocent people were made guilty by association. With the Cold War heating up, having a union strongly influenced by Communist members did not help in the negotiations. There was always a suspicion that the union, under communist influence, had more in mind than obtaining better wages and working hours. Soviet domination of the world was considered a real threat. The strike was marked with violence. Men were beaten with sawed-off axe handles and there were criminal charges laid.

In one incident, seventeen-year-old John Lawrence was dragged off his ship at the St. Gabrial Lock in the Lachine Canal: "suddenly all hell broke loose! The wheelsman on watch was attacked, beaten and thrown overboard. He would have drowned except that another crew member, a fireman, pulled him from the water." Lawrence and the watchman, named Bill, were pushed up to Notre Dame Street, onto a streetcar, and to the union office. Pushed back onto the street, he was beaten up again. In a daze, he heard his attackers say, "Look at all the blood. You killed him." "I hope I did kill the son-of-a-bitch." In the mid-1990s and after a long career as a ship's captain, Lawrence reflected on those times:

> Although the strike was appalling there were some benefits that derived from it, such as better working and living conditions, and of course more pay. However, in retrospect, the mayhem and property damage did not seem to justify the end result, for times were changing and a peaceful solution would have eventually brought the same results.

But as the events were unfolding there was no time for deep reflection or what the

Out on bail, Banks escaped to the United States, where he received protection from extradition back to Canada.

Kingston Harbour, 1950. Many ports on the Great Lakes declined after the opening of the Seaway, and have become battlegrounds between developers and citizens demanding more access to the waterfront.

historian Desmond Morton calls "understand[ing] deep continuities. People are people: they don't change overnight even if they think they do."

In 1946 the government took control of most Great Lakes shipping companies. What followed was an "affair of war," with rapidly changing partners and alliances between shipping companies, labour organizations, and the government. The government and the shipping companies were complicit in bringing Hal Banks to Canada to head up the Seafarers International Union (SIU) and finish off the Canadian Seaman's Union. By 1949 the SIU had taken over. A few years later, Hal Banks had an unofficial list of 2,000 names, men who were placed on the notorious DNS — Do Not Ship — list. Very few on the list were, in fact, Communists. Most were sailors identified as enemies of the SIU, men who had objected to corruption and having to pay bribes to get a job. Slowly — much too slowly — a case was built against Hal Banks.

In 1962 the SIU took on Upper Lakes Shipping and its owner, Jack Leitch. Leitch fought back with the loyalty of his crew and a willingness to take the company to the wall. Ships were fired upon, the *Howard L. Shaw* was bombed, and men were beaten up, but there was enough evidence to bring criminal

After World War II

charges against Hal Banks, the SIU leader. Out on bail, Banks escaped to the United States where he received protection from extradition back to Canada. Since then, there has been relative peace, with benefits for the owners and for those who serve on ships.

The shipping companies were generally good at coping with change after the war but, as always, there were external forces at work over which they had little control. Some of this was predictable, a too-familiar story of Canadian history repeating itself. This country was built by having its natural resources plundered. The furs were extracted first, followed by timber. After that the iron ore was used up. By then, Europe no longer needed as much grain, so farmers shipped their wheat west to Pacific Ocean markets. Bulk cargo, the traditional mainstay of the Great Lakes cargo ship, was drying up. There is still coal to be transported to electric generating stations but, with new legislation to protect the environment, that payload, too, will disappear.

In the 1960s, carrying freight looked so promising that some ships were fitted with side doors so that forklift trucks could move cargo between the shoreside warehouse and the hold. This idea was soon overtaken by the most profound change of all, the introduction of containerization and the TEU. A TEU is a "twenty-foot equivalent unit," a well-designed steel box that fits into and onto the deck of a specially designed ship with no waste of space. It is also intermodal, designed to be carried by different types of freight carriers. Thousands of containers are easily moved by ship across oceans, transferred to rail, and then offloaded onto trucks for regional delivery along provincial road systems.

Advances in ship design have affected docks and harbours throughout the Great Lakes. The bulker was replaced by the self-unloader, making unnecessary the complicated shore-based loading and unloading gear to move bulk cargo. The new ship technology that reduced the need for shoreside equipment was a clarion call for urban regeneration projects that focused on the adaptive use of abandoned docklands — Toronto, Kingston, and Collingwood being good examples. Other elements of the ship — the bow shape, deck layouts, rudders and propellers — were improved to help reduce operating costs. Shipyard managers appreciated the science of hydrodynamics, particularly at Collingwood Shipyards, where innovators Stuart Thoms and Jim Elder held sway. Steel was strengthened so that the internal structure could be reduced in size, allowing more stowage space. The old-fashioned triple expansion steam engine was replaced by the steam turbine engine, which disappeared in favour of the diesel engine. A new kind of ship emerged that was at home on the Lakes and at sea.

By the late 1980s three large shipyards had been closed down and only two remained, Port Arthur and Port Weller. Shipping companies also disappeared, leaving two giants, Canada Steamship Lines and Algoma Central Marine, standing above an almost empty field. According to the transportation historian Viktor Kaczkowski, "In 1945 almost one hundred per cent of the Canadian Great Lakes Fleet was steam powered. In 2005, only fifteen per cent.... In 1945 the aggregate fleet tonnage of 146 ships in carrying capacity was 685,740 tons. In 2005 the number of ships had been reduced to 55 but the aggregate carrying capacity was now 1,576,554 tons with only 9 steamships left." Steamships, with only a few exceptions, were gone, replaced by diesel-powered vessels. The surviving steamship companies were innovative and willing to adapt to new market conditions.

9

THE LINGERING LEGACY OF STEAM

By the 21st century, the majority of steamship fleets and shipbuilders have passed into history, but a few remain. Canada Steamship Lines, Upper Lakes Shipping, and Algoma Marine are among the survivors. Most of their ships no longer need complicated shore facilities; they can unload themselves. Nor do they need a large crew. The crowded forecastles of the 1930s have been replaced by more spacious quarters. "Running away to sea" is not as popular as it used to be. The shipping companies have to work hard to attract young men and women to the profession, offering many benefits. One 730-foot ship does the work of ten canallers of the 1950s. There are two large shipyards left in Ontario, strategically located at opposite ends of the Great Lakes: Pascol Engineering specializes in repair work at Thunder Bay, while Port Weller Drydock near St. Catharines is a full-service shipyard. Most of the ships are now powered by diesel engines, with a few turbine ships barely in service.

There are still a few survivors in steam: the *Canadian Leader*, built in 1967; *Canadian Provider*, 1963; *Halifax*, 1963; *James Norris* and *Montrealis*, both 1962; and *Quebecois*, 1963. The 730-foot *Canadian Leader* was built by Collingwood Shipyards. She has a Canadian General Electric

The lingering legacy of steam is also the memory of those who conducted their daily lives aboard steamships.

The Lingering Legacy of Steam

9,000-horsepower steam turbine engine. Through the Seaway she can carry 26,000 tons of cargo — grain downriver, and iron ore in the back-haul from St. Lawrence River ports. She is sailing under charter for Seaway Bulk Carriers, a partnership between two large shipping companies, Upper Lakes and Algoma. The *Canadian Leader* has an uncertain future. Her design is now considered old-fashioned, with no self-unloading gear, and the grain and iron ore trade is far from reliable. The *Halifax*, the ex-*Frankcliffe Hall*, may last longer. She was built as a bulker and then converted to a self-unloader in 1980.

The Canadian Leader. *As inevitable as the passing of the seasons, steam has given way to diesel. Only a few big steamships linger on, counting the days to their end.*

Ultimately, the same fundamental decisions about ships and trade that had to be made by John Hamilton, Donald Bethune, Hugh Richardson, and Henry Gildersleeve in the early 19th century are still faced by the 21st century shipowner. The story of steamship preservation has always been two-fold, a story of zealous individuals who were by nature unable to accept the word no and, behind these dedicated leaders, with them, and sometimes ahead of them, the hundreds of others who dipped into their pockets to donate money, influence, and thousands of hours of volunteer labour. These two groups also represent the future of steam and of maritime history preservation.

The *Segwun* is a steamboat twice born. The first *Nipissing* burned in 1886 after fifteen years of service. Her engines were installed into an iron hull brought in pieces from the Clyde, Scotland, and then riveted together at Gravenhurst. *Nipissing* (2), still a side-wheel steamship, had an up-and-down career of activity and idleness until 1924, when the Navigation Company decided to rebuild her. A year later the *Segwun* was launched. The well-built Scottish iron hull was re-used. The old engine was removed along with the paddlewheels. *Segwun* was propeller-driven, with two compound steam engines. She seemed to lead a charmed life, just surviving the Depression years of the 1930s and seeing heavier usage during World War II. The tragedy of the *Noronic* fire in 1949 brought in new ship regulations, forcing some of *Segwun's* fleetmates out of service. Eventually the owners were worn out by too many woes, including a grounding and propeller damage, and the *Segwun* was taken out of service.

Steamboats on the Lakes

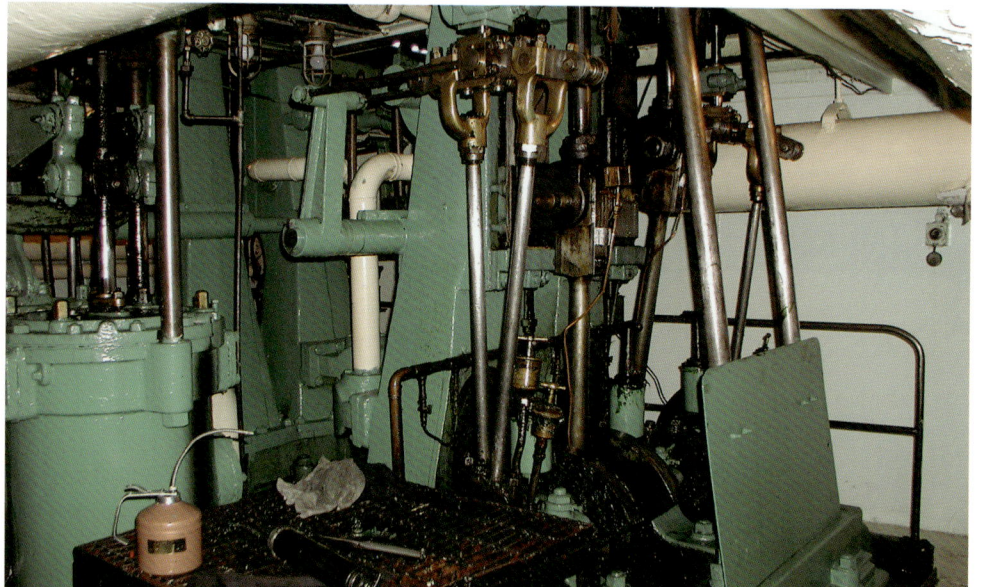

Top: The Segwun, *a miraculous survivor from the 19th century, continues to steam the Muskoka Lakes. Bottom: Segwun's triple expansion steam engine. A steam engine in motion is a testament to the ingenuity of countless steam engineers.*

The town of Gravenhurst purchased the *Segwun* and turned her into a museum ship in 1962, but she wasn't left to languish. Enthusiasts saw her potential and wanted her back in service. Among the dedicated was single-minded steam engineer John Coulter, who was instrumental in getting the steam back into the ship and returning her to glory on the Muskoka Lakes. Progress was slow until 1973, when Glen Coates and the Ontario Road Builders Association sponsored a refit. On June 1, 1974, *Segwun,* with a new hull plating (the Scots were good, but not that good) and a propeller, was launched by the Right Honourable Pierre Elliott Trudeau. Money was still needed. The province of Ontario gave $400,000 towards the cause, and eventually the total reached $1.3 million. The *Segwun* is owned by the Muskoka Steamship and Historical Society, a non-profit organization set up by the Road Builders.

The Lingering Legacy of Steam

There is a growing fleet of ships steaming out of Gravenhurst, a new museum being built, our maritime heritage being preserved — all contributing to the local economy.

At Kingston there is a different kind of steam-powered beauty, the 48-foot Edwardian yacht *Phoebe*. She was built in Kingston's inner harbour, site of the first shipbuilding on the entire Great Lakes where the French constructed four little sailing vessels in 1679. A boat-building tradition has continued on the same location for well over three hundred years, but back in 1914 the Davis Drydock Company exemplified the best standards as shipbuilders. The peak years for the firm ran from 1890 until about 1920. It specialized in medium-sized yachts, but built larger steamers as well. The 107-foot *James Swift* of 1893 was certainly one of the company's most beautiful creations. She made regular runs between Kingston and Ottawa on the Rideau Canal.

Phoebe was an act of appreciation on the part of grateful students and friends wishing to honour their teacher and mentor, Dr. John Brashear from Pittsburgh. He and his wife Phoebe owned a cottage on Lake Muskoka and, thus, the *Phoebe* and *Segwun* are soulmates; they knew each other on the same lake.

The Phoebe, *now restored, lies in wait until the day when she will steam again.*

The *Phoebe* owes much to the late Jack Telgeman, known as Mr. Steam. Jack's powers of persuasion convinced the Canadian government that the *Phoebe* should be repatriated from the U.S. as Canadian Cultural Property in 1979. In addition to granting the highly regarded designation, the Canadian government put up almost all the money to obtain the vessel. In 1985, Telgeman had the *Phoebe* steaming up the Rideau Canal to help celebrate the 100th anniversary of Parks Canada. After Jack passed from the scene, perhaps to the sailor's heaven called Fiddler's Green, the *Phoebe* sat as a static exhibit on the waterfront site of Kingston's Pump House Steam Museum. A few years later a retired engineering professor from

The propulsion steam engine for the Edmonton, *a Great Lakes ship, built at Hebburn On Tyne, England, in 1906. The few engines that remain are historic engineering artifacts.*

Queen's University, Henk Wevers, started recruiting volunteers and financial support with the help of the Marine Museum of the Great Lakes. He put together a strong team that took on the task of restoring the *Phoebe*. The boathouse rang with the sound of hammer and chisel wielded by the volunteer team, along with learned discussions about the philosophical distinctions between restoration and replication. The *Phoebe* will continue to be a testament to the outstanding craftsmanship of an earlier era and the power of steam. When, years from now, the successors of Jack Telgemen and Henk Wevers appear with that single minded-passion, the *Phoebe* will steam again.

Steam power, the telegraph, newspapers, and the railway are early and linked determinants in the success of Ontario, but this is no argument for technological determinism. Change is all about people using the resources at hand in innovative ways, and in understanding that there are ideals and ambitions that transcend politics and money. The natural resources that built the province are mostly gone and, with that, most of the ships. It was a dirty age, those glory days of steam. As late as the 1960s, a trail of smoke sitting on the horizon was a common sight. The clear cool air of Georgian Bay, Lake Huron, and Superior is no longer the home to that sooty black smudge from a ship's smokestack, a sight in the distance that would cause the heart to skip and the mind to wander. And the sound is gone, the dangerous power in those steam boilers and pistons that

The Lingering Legacy of Steam

was so gentle to the ear. Steam whistles — seeing the steam first, hearing the sound later — are a rarely experienced pleasure in the 21st century. The coal piles have disappeared from the waterfronts, as have most of the grain elevators. And yet, in places like the atomic energy plants of Bruce and Pickering, it is still steam that drives the turbines to generate electricity. Steam lingers on. For the most part it is hidden from view, but its legacy continues to serve Ontario.

Top: Midland Shipyards, 1909, where every vessel is a steamship. The ships are gone but many harbours such as this one remain on the Lakes, and can be visited. Bottom: The clear, cool air of the Great Lakes is no longer home to the evocative sooty, black smudge on the horizon from a steamship's smokestack.

List of Ships

Where possible, and in this order, I have listed the name, length, beam, depth of hold, builder, build date, and engines of the ships found in these pages. Dimensions are given in feet. There are many ways to measure a ship, including length, so keep in mind the recording of statistics is inconsistent through the nearly two-hundred-year period. Readers seeking more detailed information about the steamships are advised to consult the publications and web sites listed in the Sources section of this book.

Accommodation. 85 x 16. Built by J. Bruce at the H. Logan yard, Montreal, and launched August 19, 1809. Engine cast at St. Maurice Forges, Trois-Rivières. Used only 1809 and 1810 seasons; laid up at Boucherville until at least early 1812. First Canadian steamboat.

A. E. Ames. 246 x 37 x 21. Built by Northumberland Shipbuilding Co., Newcastle, England, 1903. Engines 201/2-33-59 x 36 by Wallsend Slipway Co. War loss 1940.

Alberta. 264 x 38 x 23. Built by C. Connell & Co., Whiteinch, Scotland, and launched July 12, 1883. Engine 35-70 x 48 by D. Rowan & Co., Glasgow. Passenger & freight, freight-only latterly.

Alciope. c.140 x 48. Built Niagara, Ont., and launched April 22, 1828. First engine (from *Frontenac*) by Boulton & Watt, London, England; rebuilt by J. D. Ward, Montreal. Hull rebuilt to schooner *Birmingham* winter 1834–35; wrecked November 11, 1835, Oswego, New York.

Adelaide. c.120 x 40. Built by Lovering, Chippewa, Ont., and launched June 9, 1832. Engine by Boulton & Watt, London, originally in *Frontenac*. First Canadian steamboat on Lake Erie.

Algoma. Built by Aitken & Mansell, Kelvinhaugh, Scotland, and launched July 31, 1883. Engine 35-70 x 48 by D. Rowan & Co., Glasgow. Cut apart Montreal; crossed Lake Ontario on pontoons with difficulty owing to autumn storms. Reassembled at Buffalo, wintered at Port Colborne. First of 3 new sisters to enter service: first voyage from Owen Sound, August 5, 1884. Wrecked Isle Royale, July 11, 1885, 37 killed. Engine to *Manitoba*.

America. 141 x 19 x 9. Built by Niagara Harbour & Dock Co., and launched May 1, 1842. Engines; 401/2 x 96 by builder. Sank at dock, Kingston, October 23, 1874; condemned, broken up.

Asia. 137 x 28 x 7. Built by M. Simpson, St. Catharines, and launched August 19, 1873. Sank in storm September 14, 1882, Byng Inlet, Ont. (148 killed). "Not in proper ballast trim."

Assiniboia. 336 x 44 x 37. Built by Fairfield Shipbuilding & Engineering Co., Glasgow, and launched June 25, 1907. Engine 231/2-34-481/2 x 70 by builder. Destroyed by fire near Philadelphia, Pennsylvania, September 11, 1969.

Athabasca / Athabaska. 263 x 38 x 23. Built by Aitken & Mansell, Glasgow, 1883. First engine 35-70 x 48 by D. Rowan & Co., Glasgow. Laid up 1939.

Barge 137. 351 x 45 x 22. Built Superior, Wisconsin, 1896.

Belleville. See *Spartan*.

Blue Cross. 255 x 44 x 10. Built for Red Barge Line as *Redhead*. Built by Canadian Vickers Ltd., Montreal, as barge; motorized 1934. Bulk freighter, rebuilt tanker 1940.

Britannia. 109 x 21 x 8 approx. Built by Ewen, Kingston, and launched late December 1832. Engine by Bennett & Henderson, Montreal.

Cambria. See **Champion**.

Canada. 127 x 22. Built in Toronto 1826; wrecked.

Canada. Dimensions unknown. Built by Weeks, Prescott, Ont., and launched mid-May 1841. Sank at dock, Kingston, October 17, 1855; abandoned. Known as "Canada No. 1."

Canadian Beaver. 250 x 43 x 26. Built Kingston Shipyards, 1919.

Canadian Leader. 730 x 75 x 39. Built Collingwood Shipyards as the *Feux-Follets,* 1967. Engine, Canadian General Electric 9,000-hp steam turbine.

Canadian Provider. 730 x 75 x 39. Built Collingwood Shipyards as *Murray Bay*, 1963. Engine 9,000-hp John Inglis steam turbine engine. New name after acquired by Upper Lakes Shipping.

Canadian Rover. 251 x 44. Built Collingwood Shipyards, 1920;

List of Ships

to Japan and named *Tosei Maru*, 1937; torpedoed by Allied Forces.

Car of Commerce. 163 x 30 x 5. Built by J. Goudie, Montreal, and launched October 7, 1815. Wrecked August 26, 1822, St. Mary's Current (Montreal).

Caspian. See *Passport*. 1898.

Cayuga. 305 x 37 x 15. Built by Canadian Shipbuilding Co., Toronto, and launched March 3, 1906. Engines 171/2-25-36-52 x 30 by builders; laid up 1951–53; back in service.

Champion. 131 x 23 x 11. Built by G. T. Davie, Lévis, Que., 1877. Engine 40 x 81 (maker unknown).

Charlotte. 130 x 18 x 8. Owned by H. Gildersleeve, Kingston. Built by H. Gildersleeve, Ernestown, Ont., and launched April 22, 1818. Engine by Ward Bros., Montreal. Used Prescott–Bay of Quinte. Condemned 1828 and abandoned.

Chicora. 221 x 26 x 11. Built by Lairds, Birkenhead, England, 1864. Engines (2) 52 x 48 (oscillating) by W. C. Miller, Birkenhead; "New machinery throughout" 1887; re-engined 1904, from *Toronto*. Originally blockade runner *Let Her B* (one of a trio, with *Let Her Go* and *Let Her Rip*). Left Liverpool April 5, 1864, made at least 12 blockade-running voyages. For sale at Halifax, 1865, as *Chicora*. First arrival at Toronto early June 1868.

Chief Justice Robinson. c.167 x 23. Built by Niagara Harbour & Dock Co. and launched September 10, 1842. Last used 1856; converted to "a respectable scow" (*Globe*) by Shickluna, St. Catharines.

Chippewa. 308 x 36 x 14 (width over paddle boxes 68'). Built by Hamilton Bridge Co., Hamilton, and launched May 2, 1893. Engine 75 x 132 by W. & A. Fletcher, Hoboken, N. J.

City of Hamilton. 156 x 24 x 9. Built by P. Beaupré, Bath, Ont., and launched December 25, 1850. Not used after about 1874; still lying at Garden Island, 1881.

City of Kingston. 230 x 38 x 11. Built by Davie Shipbuilding & Repairing Co., Lévis, Que., 1925. Engine 18-30-50 x 36 by Richardson Westgarth & Co., Hartlepool, England. Retired 1958; scrapped Lévis, Que., winter 1961–62.

City of Toronto. (probably never ran as *Racine*) 147 x 23 x 12. Built by Niagara Harbour & Dock Co. and launched December 31, 1840. Engines (2) 46 x 144 by Ward & Brush, Montreal. Sank winter 1877–78 at Collingwood; abandoned.

Clermont. 133 x 18 x 7. Built 1807, Charles Brown, N.Y. Boulton & Watt steam engine, 24-inch cylinder.

Cobourg. 150 x 25 x 11 approx. Built by Wm. Hathaway & C. McIntosh, Cobourg, Ont., and launched June 3, 1833. Engines (2) by Sheldon & Dutcher (York Foundry), Toronto. Blown from moorings in gale October 25, 1844, Niagara, beached opposite shore; probably not used afterwards.

Columbian. 175 x 34 x 9. Built by Delaware River Iron Shipbuilding & Engine Works, Chester, Pennsylvania, 1892. Engine 121/2-19-30 x 15 by builder. To Kingston "for disposal" 1934; became floating hotel, Morrisburg, 1936; soon became oil barge. Hulk eventually part of breakwater, Queen City Yacht Club.

Commerce. 140 x 22 x 8. Built by Niagara Harbour & Dock Co. and launched May 27, 1843. Engine 54 x 132 by builders. Renamed *Eclipse* after beating (barely) American *Lady of the Lake* in Niagara–Toronto challenge race.

Commodore Barrie. c.144 x 38 x 9. Built by Ewen, Kingston, and launched May 9, 1834. Engines (2) by Ward Foundry, Montreal. Wrecked in collision with schooner *Canada* April 30, 1842, South Bay, Prince Edward County, Ont.

Coverdale. 639 x 67 x 30. Built 1950, Midland Shipyards Ltd. Engine (Skinner Uniflow, enclosed), 4 (4@27) x 30.

D. D. Calvin. 166 x 32 x 15. Built by Roney, Garden Island, and launched September 11, 1883. Engine 24-50 x 36 by Globe Iron Works, Cleveland. Destroyed by fire April 11, 1910, Garden Island.

Donald Stewart. 250 x 43 x 19. Built by Smiths Dock Co., South Bank-on-Tees, England, and launched April 14, 1923. Engine 16-26-44 x 33 by builders. Torpedoed September 3, 1942, near Strait of Belle Isle, Gulf of St. Lawrence; cargo of aviation fuel exploded.

D. R. Van Allen. 136 x 26 x 10. Built by Chisholm & Simpson, Chatham and launched June 13, 1874. Engine 23 x 24 by Hyslop & Ronald, Chatham. Condemned 1920 and broken up at Port Arthur.

Durham boats. c.50 x 8. Open boat; used oars, poles, and sail; often towed upstream around rapids carrying cargo and passengers. Carried up to 20 tons.

Edmonton. 249 x 43 x 21. Built by Robert Stephenson & Co., Hebburn-on-Tyne, England, 1906. Engine 17-28-46 x 33 by

Steamboats on the Lakes

North East Marine Engineering Works, Newcastle, England. Retired 1958. Scrapped Lévis, Que., 1961.

Erin. 142 x 26 x 13. Built by Shickluna Bros., St. Catharines, and launched July 28, 1881. Engine 24 x 30 by G. N. Oill, St. Catharines. Sunk in collision with *John B. Cowle*, May 31, 1906, St. Clair River, 5 killed.

Eugene C. Roberts (named *Portadoc* 1939). 253 x 43 x 18. Built by Cammell Laird, Birkenhead, England, and launched March 5, 1924. Engine 16-27-44 x 33 by builders. Requisitioned for war use 1940. War loss April 4, 1941, North Africa.

Europa. 224 x 28 x 13. Built by E. Harrison & Co., Hamilton and launched July 27, 1954. Engine 60 x 132 by J. Gartshore, Dundas, Ont.

Frank A. Sherman. 681 x 73 x 37. Built Port Weller Shipyards, 1958. Engine, 7,500-hp steam turbine.

Frank B. Baird. 253 x 43 x 18. Built by Napier & Miller, Glasgow, Scotland. Engine 16-27-44 x 33 (maker unknown). Requisitioned for war use, 1940. War loss May 22, 1942, North Atlantic.

Frankcliffe Hall. 730 x 75 x 39. Built Davie Shipbuilding, Lévis, 1962. Engine, single 9,000-hp steam turbine engine.

Frontenac. c.150 x 30 x 12. Owned by Mrs. L. Finkle, Ernestown, Ont.; to J. & R. Hamilton, St. Catharines, 1827. Begun by Teabout & Chapman, completed by H. Gildersleeve, Ernestown, Ont., 1816. Engine by Boulton & Watt. Sailed from Kingston for scrapping August 18, 1827; run onto beach at Niagara for removal of engine. Later broke adrift, picked up and towed in; destroyed by fire September 29, 1827.

Glencorrie. 250 x 43 x 18. Built by Swan Hunter & Wigham Richardson, Wallsend, England, 1923. First vessel (with *Prescodoc*) through St. Lawrence Seaway May 2, 1959. Converted to gas drilling barge *Nordrill*, 1961. Scrapped at Port Colborne, 1977.

Glencova. 255 x 42 x 21. Built by Midland Shipbuilding Co. and launched December 21, 1920. Engine 18-30-50 x 42 by Frontier Iron Works, Detroit (made 1889) from United States *Major*. Requisitioned for war use 1940–1953; repowered with diesel engine 1955. Scrapped Duluth 1970.

Gleneagles. Built by Midland Shipbuilding Co. and launched August 26, 1925. Engine 21.5-41.5-72 x 48 by Hooven Owens Rentschler, Hamilton, Ohio (World War I surplus). Converted from bulk freighter to self-unloader winter 1962–63, Port Arthur. Scrapped Windsor, Ont., 1984.

Gleniffer. 546 x 60 x 28. Built by Midland Shipbuilding Co. and launched November 18, 1924. Engine 241/2-411/2-72 x 48 by Hooven Owens Renschler, Hamilton, Ohio (World War I surplus). Scrapped Castellon, Spain, 1969.

Glenlinnie. 252 x 43 x 18. Built by Swan Hunter & Wigham Richardson, Wallsend, England, 1923. Requisitioned for war use 1941. War loss February 23, 1942.

Glenmohr. 621 x 70 x 25. Built by Midland Shipbuilding Co., 1926. Engine 251/2-411/2-72 x 48 by Hooven Owens & Rentschler, Hamilton, Ohio. 1926 renamed at first wrongly *Lemoine*, corrected after nine days to *LeMoyne* (August 11–20, 1926). Officially opened Welland Canal August 6, 1932. Scrapped Santander, Spain, 1969.

Great Britain. 147 x 23 x 12. Built by Brown & Bell, Prescott, Ont., and launched October 16, 1830. Engines (2) by Bennett & Henderson. Powerful: towed 15 schooners and a Durham boat upstream Prescott to Kingston, arriving May 16, 1832. Wrecked August 1846, Burlington Bay Canal.

Halifax. Formerly the *Frankcliffe Hall*, converted to a self-unloader in 1980. 730 x 75 x 39. See *Frankcliffe Hall*.

Hamonic. 350 x 50 x 24. Built by Collingwood Shipbuilding Co. and launched November 26, 1908. Engine 24-35-52-80 x 42 by builder. Destroyed by fire July 17, 1945, Sarnia.

Hochelaga. 639 x 67 x 30. Built 1949, Collingwood Shipyards Ltd. Engine (Skinner Uniflow, enclosed), ERS: 4 (4@27), 30, Can. Vickers Ltd. (Designs of Skinner Eng. Co., Erie, Pa.)

Howard L. Shaw. 428 x 52 x 28. Built by American Shipbuilding, Lorrain, Ohio, 1900. Used as breakwater, Ontario Place, Toronto, 1969.

Huronic. 321 x 43 x 23. Built by Collingwood Shipbuilding Co., launched September 12, 1901. Engine 26-42-70 x 42 by John Inglis & Sons, Toronto.

Inter-Ocean. 103 x 23 x 6. Built by C. Smiley, South River, Lake Nipissing, 1881. Engine 14 x 16, made "part in Buffalo, part in Peterborough" (per Registry; no further details). Said to be first steamer on Lake Nipissing.

List of Ships

James Norris. 664 x 67 x 35. Built Midland Shipbuilding Co., converted to a self-unloader 1980–81. Engine Skinner Uniflow, Canadian Vickers Montreal.

James Whalen. 108 x 24 x 13. Built by Bertram Engineering Works, Toronto 1905. Engine 20-40 x 36 by builder. Tug. Permanently moored at Thunder Bay, Ont., as *James Whalen*.

James Swift. Built by M. R. Davis & Sons, Kingston, 1893. Engine 9-16 x 12 by D. McEwen & Sons, Kingston.

J. H. Plummer. 246 x 37 x 22. Built by Armstrong Whitworth & Co., Walker on Tyne, England 1903. Engine 201/2-33-54 x 36 by Wallsend Slipway Co., Wallsend, England.

John B. Richards. built by Napier & Miller, Old Kilpatrick, Scotland, and launched March 12, 1925. Engine 17-281/2-47 x 33 (maker unknown).

John S. Pillsbury. 253 x 43 x 18. Built by Earles Shipbuilding & Engineering Co., Hull, England, 1926. Engine 17-28-46 x 33 (maker unknown). Scrapped Port Dalhousie, Ont., 1964.

Keewatin. 336 x 44 x 24. Built by Fairfield Shipbuilding & Engineering Co., Glasgow, Scotland. Engine 231/2-34-481/2-70 x 45 by builder. Laid up 1965, to Saugatuck, Michigan, as floating museum, 1967.

Kingston. 288 x 36 x 13 (width over paddle boxes 66'). Built by Bertram Engineering Works, Toronto, and launched January 19, 1901. Engine 28-44-74 x 72 by builder.

Lady Colborne. 173 x 20 x 10 (width over paddle boxes 39'). Built by Shea & Merritt, Montreal, and launched May 18, 1839. First engine 10 x 120 by Molson's Foundry, Montreal; replaced 1855 with new engine, same dimensions, maker unknown.

LeMoyne. see *Glenmohr*.

Lord Sydenham. 197 x 25, named *Lord Sydenham* a year after it was lauched.

Macassa. 154 x 24 x 16. Built by Wm. Hamilton & Co., Port Glasgow, Scotland; rebuilt to 178 x 24 x 16 by Collingwood Shipbuilding Co., 1905. Engines (2) 11-18-29 x 22 by W. Kemp, Govan, Scotland.

Maggie Hunter. Great Lakes schooner.

Magnet. 173 x 26 x 11. Built by Niagara Harbour & Dock Co. and launched July 3, 1847. First engine 44 x 120 by builder. Stranded June 5, 1883, Cedar Island, near Thessalon, Ont.; refloated. Stranded August 12, 1903, running Long Sault Rapids.

Majestic. 209 x 35 x 13. Built Collingwood, 1895. Engine 28-54 x 36 by J. Inglis, Toronto. Formally opened Canadian Sault Ste. Marie lock September 7, 1895. Destroyed by fire December 15, 1915, Point Edward, Ont.

Malsham. 155 x 30 x 11. Built by H. Logan, Montreal, and launched September 20, 1814. Engine by Boulton & Watt, London, England, to *St. Lawrence*. Officially registered as "square sterned vefsel [sic] worked by steam with wheels or flyers at each side."

Manitoba. 303 x 38 x 15. Built by Polson Iron Works, Owen Sound, Ont., and launched May 4, 1889. Engine 30-64 x 48 by D. Rowan & Co., from *Algoma*. Carried 300 passengers.

Maple Leaf. 173 x 25 x 19. Built by Kingston Marine Railway (G. Thurston) and launched June 18, 1851. Engine from *Sovereign*. Left for United States service August 14, 1862. Destroyed by fire and sunk by "torpedo," April 1, 1864, St. Johns River, near Jacksonville, Florida.

Mathewston. 530 x 58 x 27. Built by Port Arthur Shipbuilding Co., 1922. Engine 251/2-41-67 x 42 (maker unknown). Scrapped Vado, Italy, 1970.

Mattawan. 50 x 10 x 3. Built 1876. Engine 7 x 9 by Chaffey Bros., Portsmouth, Ont. Built to run Mattawa-Deux Rivières: "only steamer able to run up the rapids." Taken to Lake Temiskaming 1882; back again 1886.

Modjeska. 178 x 31 x 12. Built by Napier, Shanks & Bell, Dumbarton, Scotland, 1889. Engines (2) 15-24-40 x 27 by Dunsmuir & Jackson, Govan, Scotland. Ran into breakwater in fog, July 7, 1924, Western Gap, Toronto; laid up until sold to Owen Sound.

Montreal. 332 x 43 x 15 (width over paddle boxes 76'). Built by Bertram Engineering Works, Toronto, and launched February 3, 1902. Engine 32-53-88 x 78 by builder. Completed May 1905. Destroyed by fire December 18, 1926, near Sorel.

Montrealais. 730 x 75 x 39. Built in two sections: bow at Davie and Sons, Lévis, 1961, stern section, Canadian Vickers, 1961; sections joined at Lévis in October 1961. (Launched as *Montrealer* and name changed in 1962). Powered by steam turbine engine.

Steamboats on the Lakes

New Era. 172 x 39 x 9. Built by G. Thurston at Fowler's Yard, Kingston, and launched about June 1, 1848. First engines probably 44 x 120 (maker unknown); after 1862, 40 x 126, probably from *City of Hamilton*. Destroyed by fire March 20, 1968, Kingston.

Nipissing. 110 x 18 x 7 (width over paddle boxes 31'). Launched July 24, 1871. Engine 26 x 72 by Davidson & Doran, Kingston. Destroyed by fire August 3, 1886, near Port Cockburn.

Nipissing / Segwun. 125 x 21 x 8. Built by M. Simpson, Gravenhurst, 1887. Paddle engine 26 x 72 by Davidson & Doran, Kingston, from old *Nipissing*; screw engines (2) 10-20 x 14 by Doty Engine Works. Laid up 1914–25, 1958–81. Still in service.

Noronic. 362 x 52 x 25. Built by Western Drydock & Shipbuilding Co., Port Arthur. Engine 4 cyl. 3-exp. 29 1/2-47 1/2-58-58 x 42 (maker uncertain). Fabricated in Cleveland. Widened with "bulges" 1915 to improve stability; previously had to carry pig-iron ballast. Destroyed by fire September 16, 1949, Toronto, 119 killed.

Norseman. 154 x 26 x 10 (width over paddle boxes 45'). Built by A. Cantin, Montreal, and launched June 4, 1868. Rebuilt to 175 x 43 x 10 by Davis & Sons, Kingston, 1891. Engine 36 x 120 by E. E. Gilbert, Montreal; rebuilt by Kingston Foundry, 1891. Named *North King*, 1891. Broken up.

North King. see *Norseman*.

Northumberland. 220 x 33 x 20. Built by Wigham Richardson & Co., Newcastle, England, 1891. Engines (2) 17 1/2-27 1/2-46 x 33 (maker unknown). Destroyed by fire while fitting out, June 2, 1949, Port Dalhousie.

Ontario. 110 x 24 x 8. Built at Sackets Harbour by Ashel Roberts, 1817. Engine low-pressure cross-head beam engine by Daniel Dod, New Jersey, 21 hp.

Passport. 172 x 25 x 10. Built by W. McCausland at Kingston Marine Railway and launched December 11, 1846. Rebuilt 1906. First engines (2) 42 x 120 by Ward & Brush, Montreal; after 1902, 42 x 120 by G. A. Pontbriand, Sorel.

Pathfinder. 136 x 18 x 10 (yacht). Owned by J. Playfair, Midland, 1921; to Dominion Government, 1929; to Yacht Pathfinder Ltd., Toronto, 1934; to R. T. French, Midland, 1947. Removed from Register 1959; broken up.

Pathfinder and **Playfair**. 60 x 15 x 10. Built Kingston Shipyards 1963 and Canadian Dredge and Dock 1973, sailing rig: brigantine, in service as a leadership training vessel for youth.

Phoebe. 41 x 8 x 3. Built Kingston, Ont., 1914, preserved as a museum ship, Kingston, Ont.

Ploughboy. 170 x 28 x 8. Built by J. McDermott, Chatham, Ont., and launched June 24, 1851. Engine 42 x 48 by Ward Bros., Montreal. Destroyed by fire, June 3, 1870, Detroit, during conversion work for intended passenger service Port Stanley–Cleveland.

Portadoc. see *Eugene C. Roberts*.

Prince of Wales. 135 x 20 x 6 (width over paddle boxes 31'). Built by Kingston Marine Railway and launched December 22, 1841. First engine from *Sir James Kempt*. Sank June 1, 1855, head of Galops Rapids, taken to Hatter's Bay (Portsmouth) and abandoned. Engine salvaged 1863.

Quebec. 350 x 70 x 19. Built by Davie Shipbuilding & Repairing Co., Lévis, 1928. Engine 4-cyl. 3-exp. 28-38-44-44 x 36.

Quebecois. 730 x 76 x 39. Built in two parts at Canadian Vickers: stern September 1962, bow November 1962. Engine steam turbine.

Queen Charlotte. 130 x 18 x 8. Built by H. Gildersleeve, Ernestown, Ont., and launched April 22, 1818. Engine by Ward Bros., Montreal. Used Prescott–Bay of Quinte. Condemned 1828 and abandoned.

Queen Victoria. 130 x 20 x 7. Built by Niagara Harbour & Dock Co. and launched April 4, 1838. Engines (2) 28 x 72 by builder. Used on Lake Ontario.

Racine. see *City of Toronto*.

Ralph Budd. 382 x 50 x 26. Built by Great Lakes Engineering Works, Ecorse, Michigan, 1905. Engine 21-30-43 1/2-63 x 42 by builder. Scrapped Hamilton, 1966.

Rapids King. 239 x 41 x 10. Built by Canadian Shipbuilding Co., Toronto, 1907. Engines (2) 4-cyl. 3-exp. 15 1/2-24-30-30 x 22 by builder. Intended to run St. Lawrence rapids but drew too much water and became a "white elephant." Tried Rochester–Murray Canal–Kingston–Alexandria Bay service 1926.

Rapids Prince. 197 x 37 x 8. Engines (2) 4-cyl. 3-exp. 12 1/2-20-22-22 x 16 by John Inglis, Toronto. Stranded July 30, 1922, Lachine Rapids, aground six weeks.

Rapids Queen. see *Columbian*.

List of Ships

HMS *Revenge*. Built Vickers (UK) 1916. Battleship, 8 15-inch guns, 620 x 88 x 33. Engine Parsons turbines.

St. George. 159 x 26 x 11. Built by F. D. Merritt, Montreal, and launched November 19, 1831. Engines (2) 96" stroke, by Ward Bros., Montreal. Broke cylinder and crank of one engine September 9, 1837, Pte. aux Trembles; out for some time.

Sarnian. 332 x 42 x 27. Built by Cleveland Shipbuilding Co., 1895. Engine 20-33-54 x 40 by builder. Wrecked December 10, 1943, Keewenaw Point, Lake Superior; salvaged for scrap, 1947.

Segwun. 125 x 21 x 8. Built by M. Simpson, Gravenhurst, 1887. Paddle engine 26 x 72 by Davidson & Doran, Kingston, from old *Nipissing*; screw engines (2) 10-20 x 14 by Doty Engine Works. Laid up 1914–25, 1958–81.

Simcoe. See *Glencorrie*.

Sir James Dunn. 639 x 67 x 30. Built Port Arthur Shipbuilding, 1952. Pt. Arthur SB. Co. Ltd. Engine (Skinner Uniflow, enclosed), 4 (4@27) 30, Can. Vickers Ltd.

Spartan. 176 x 28 x 11 (Belleville, 1905) . Built by E. E. Gilbert at Cantin's yard, Montreal, and launched November 1, 1864. First engine 42 x 108 by E. E. Gilbert. Rebuilt with new cylinder 1875; compounded 1891. After 1918, 43 x 108 by G. A. Pontbriand, Sorel.

Stadacona. 639 x 67 x 30 (Thunder Bay). Built Port Arthur Shipyards, 1952. Engine Skinner Uniflow (4@27), Canadian Vickers Ltd.

Stormount. 249 x 43 x 21. Built by A. McMillan & Son, Dumbarton, Scotland, 1907. Engine 201/2-33-54 x 36 by Muir & Houston, Glasgow. Requisitioned for war use, 1915. Wrecked in fog, June 20, 1916, Gull Ledge, Marie Joseph Island, N. S.

Swiftsure. 120 x 24. Built by H. Logan, Montreal, 1812. Engine by Boulton & Watt, London, England, to *New Swiftsure*. Late arrival of engines delayed trial trip until April 25, 1813.

Thunder Bay. see *Stadacona*.

Toronto. 269 x 36 x 14. Built by Bertram Engine Works, Toronto, and launched June 21, 1898. Engine 28-44-74 x 72 by builder. Boilers condemned 1939 and vessel laid up; broken up; 1947.

Toronto. c. 87 x 19 x 8. Launched April 23, 1825. Built on "Mr. Annesley's improved plan": bow and stern same shape, had no ribs. Hull made of several layers of thin boards alternately lengthwise and abeam, with oiled paper between.

Transit (*Constitution*). 130 x 26 x 8. Built by Chisholm, Oakville, Ont., 1821. Engine by Ward, Montreal.

T.R. McLagan. 714 x 70 x 37. Built Midland Shipyards, 1954. Engines two 9,000-hp turbines, Westinghouse Elec. Co.

TR trawlers. 125 x 23 x 13. Various Canadian builders between 1917 and 1919.

Turbinia. 250 x 33 x 13. Built by Hawthorne Leslie & Co., Hebburnon-on-Tyne, England, and launched March 1, 1904. Triple-screw turbine powered, H.P. on centre shaft. L.P. on wing shafts. Towed to Toronto for refitting, 1923; to St. Lawrence, 1925, but laid up, 1928, and broken up, 1937.

United Kingdom. see *Alciope*.

Venetia. 201 x 27 x 16. Built by R.W. Hawthorne & Co., Leith, Scotland, 1903. Yacht. Broken up c. 1963.

Walk-in-the-Water. 145 x 32. Built Noah Brown, Black Rock, NY, 1818.

Wanda III. 94 x 12 x 6. Built by Polson Iron Works, Toronto, 1915. Engine by builder. Yacht. Moved Muskoka to Lake of Bays 1930; back again 1992. Fully restored and operational (steam).

Waubuno. 135 x 19 x 7. Wrecked November 22, 1879, "The Haystacks," 20 miles south of Parry Sound, remains not found until next spring. "Found" again September 1897.

Wenona. 67 x 10. Built Prescott, Ont., 1905.

Westmount. 248 x 42 x 21. Built by Swan & Hunter, Wallsend, England, 1903. Engine 21-35-58 x 39 by North Eastern Marine Engineering Co., Wallsend.

HMCS *Weyburn*. 205 x 33 x 11. Built Port Arthur Shipyards, 1941. Lost at sea, 1943.

William IV. 135 x 25 x 10. Built by J. Wood, Gananoque, and launched October 29, 1931. First engine by Ward Bros. Caught by freeze-up, December 1853, Lachine.

HMCS *Ypres*. 130 x 23 x 13. Built by Polson Iron Works, Toronto, 1917.

A Quick Tour of the Ontario Coastline of the Great Lakes

Ontario deserves to be called a maritime province. It has a rich history associated with coastal communities, canals, fishing, shipbuilding, engineering, watercraft, transportation, and, most important, individuals whose lives were centred on the water. The list of sites I include in my "tour" is by necessity very short and subjective, for the most part including places along the Great Lakes I have personally visited, and even then not all, particularly the lighthouses. The routes are along coastal roads, so I recommend travel by bicycle, by car, or on foot. Ontario is a place with a long coastline, so the expected travel time might extend over a few years! The mood of the shoreline and its many towns and villages cannot be appreciated at high speed.

Canals and Routes

Canals constitute a special category of living history because they are accessible to the traveller by car, on foot, or by bicycle. Many are still in operation. Visit most of these and you will qualify as a canal-aholic, which is not a bad thing to be. In the maritime world, "up" means moving west through the Great Lakes against the current, which is why Thunder Bay on Lake Superior is at the "head of the Lakes." Down is with the flow, easterly and towards Montreal. Montreal is a traditional terminus of the Great Lakes transportation system.

The route along the Lachine Canal in Montreal has been developed into a magnificent eleven-kilometre urban park. As a National Historic Site, it is well interpreted and very visitor-friendly. A few miles to the west at Pointe-des-Cascades you will find one of the most canal-intensive places in Canada. Be warned — it is not interpreted and a bit raw, but well worth the walking it demands. You can usually pick up a pamphlet at the Parc Maritime Museum; small, run by volunteers, full of fine models of canals, solid information, and interesting artifacts.

At Pointe-des-Cascades you can see the location and often the remnants and routes of the "rigolet" canal, 1749–1779; the Faucille canal, 1779–1805; the Trou-du-Moulin canal, 1779–1805; and the Rocher-Fendu canal, 1779–1845. These are the canals that the first settlers from across the Atlantic had to endure in their movement west. By travelling west to Coteau you can cross the river and look at both the old and new Beauharnois Canals. At Valleyfield, follow the old Beauharnois Canal route towards Montreal, and then, at the most easterly point, swing south to be overwhelmed by the new Beauharnois section of the Seaway.

A road runs along the old Soulanges Canal between Pointe-des-Cascades and Coteau-du-Lac. Along that route at Coteau-du-Lac is a National Historic Site devoted to the 18th-century forerunner of the modern-day St. Lawrence Seaway. The Soulanges Canal starts at Pointe-des-Cascades just a few feet from the local convenience store that sensibly sells beer and spirits, while across the road is Le Parc des Anchors. There are more than forty anchors and pieces of equipment in this park. The Soulanges Canal, opened in 1899 and closed down in 1959, is the youngster on this side of the river, with many features intact and a good road and bicycle path that follows its entire length. It was a replacement for the first Beauharnois Canal in operation from 1845 to 1899. The canal engineers did not like the old Beauharnois route, but local politics and patronage were too strong; half a century later, with the opening of the Soulanges, they had their satisfaction. Their victory was short-lived. A new Beauharnois Canal was built after World War II as part of the St. Lawrence Seaway.

Further west there is a good observation point on the St. Lawrence River section of the Seaway at the Iroquois Lock. This is a favourite spot for that special breed of observer called the ship buff. In England such devotees are affectionately referred to as anoraks. The river road along the south shore of the St. Lawrence River will take you close to sections of the older canal.

The Rideau Canal, dating from 1832, is in full operation and a potential World Heritage Site. It is a remarkable piece of 19th-century engineering that is almost entirely intact. The entrances to the canal at Ottawa in the north and at Kingston Mills in the south near Kingston are good places to start. Both settings are spectacular. The Parliament buildings and the Château Laurier are on either side, as the canal locks descend to the Ottawa River, while the Kingston Mills locks are cut through a rocky gorge. There is road access to the locks between Ottawa and Kingston, and these are in beautiful settings.

Sections of the Trent Severn Canal are accessible. Of particular interest are the hydraulic locks, giant boat elevators, at Peterborough. While there, visit the Canadian Canoe Museum — a broadly based collection, well presented, that takes the beauty of the canoe and its influence in the formative years of Canada as a starting point.

A Quick Tour of the Ontario Coastline of the Great Lakes

Certainly one of the most dramatic observation points for watching ships "lock through" on the Welland Canal is the observation platform at Lock 3, with the St. Catharines Museum adjacent to the lock. Many of the exhibits are devoted to the canal, and at the book store there are good, detailed visiting guides to the old and new Welland Canals. At Port Dalhousie on Lake Ontario you can see architectural reminders, including an early lock, of the canal town it once was. At the southerly end of the Welland Canal, which is Port Colborne, there is the Port Colborne Historical and Marine Museum and Heritage Village. The Museum interprets and exhibits the history of Port Colborne and the Welland Canal.

There is a National Historic Site at Sault Ste. Marie devoted to the canal finished in 1895. This canal was the last link in an all-Canadian navigation system stretching from the St. Lawrence River to Lake Superior. On the Soo waterfront at the Roberta Bondar Marina is the preserved MS *Norgoma* that served in the 1950s and 60s as a passenger and freight vessel along the "Turkey Trail."

Lachine Canal National Historic Site of Canada
Parks Canada
200 René-Lévesque Boulevard West
West Tour, 6th Floor
Montreal QC H2Z 1X4
Tel: (514) 283-6054
Web site: http://www.pc.gc.ca/

Coteau-du-Lac National Historic Site of Canada
308A Chemin du Fleuve
Coteau-du-Lac QC J0P 1B0
Tel: (450) 763-5631
Web site: http://www.pc.gc.ca/lhn-nhs/qc/coteaudulac/index_e.asp

Rideau Canal National Historic Site
34A Beckwith Street South
Smiths Falls ON K7A 2A8
Tel: (613) 283-5170
Web site: http://www.pc.gc.ca/lhn-nhs/on/rideau/index_e.asp

The Canadian Canoe Museum
910 Monaghan Road
Peterborough ON K9J 5K4
Tel: (705) 748-9153, toll free 1-866-34-CANOE (22663)
Web site: http://www.canoemuseum.net/

St. Catharines Museum, Welland Canals Centre
R.R. #6, 1932 Welland Canals Parkway (formerly Government Road)
St. Catharines ON L2R 7K6
Tel: (905) 984-8880; toll-free 1-800-305-5134
Fax (905) 984-6910

Port Colborne Historical and Marine Museum and Heritage Village
General Inquiries: 280 King Street (Box 572)
Port Colborne ON L3K 5X8
Tel: (905) 834-7604
Fax: (905) 834-6198
Web site: http://city.portcolborne.on.ca/visitinghere/attractions/museum/

Sault Ste. Marie Canal National Historic Site of Canada
1 Canal Drive
Sault Ste. Marie ON P6A 6W4
Tel: (705) 941-6262
Web site: http://www.pc.gc.ca/lhn-nhs/on/ssmarie/index_e.asp

MS *Norgoma*
Located at the marina in Roberta Bondar Park and Pavilion complex, Sault Ste. Marie
Tel: (705) 759-5310
Web site: http://www.norgoma.org/main.html

Lake Ontario

Kingston, at the foot of the Great Lakes, was established as a port city by the French in the 17th century and later developed as a naval and military centre by the British. Many limestone buildings and military structures survive. Kingston is where sail and steam began on the Lakes. The Marine Museum of the Great Lakes, in historic shipyard buildings, is located on the waterfront. The resplendent, stone Gildersleeve House, formerly owned by the "father of steam navigation," is on King Street only a few blocks from the downtown core. Portsmouth Village, dominated by the walls of the Kingston Penitentiary (known locally as KP) was the site of the 1976 Olympic Sailing events. Kingston is now a major yachting centre.

To the west is Prince Edward County, an island with Lake Ontario on one side and the Bay of Quinte on the other. Many of the small villages and towns survive from the 19th century, Picton being a very good example. South Bay was an anchorage of refuge for schooners escaping westerly gales on Lake Ontario. At the head of the bay is the well-positioned and volunteer-run Mariners Museum.

Take the bridge off the County and follow the shore road west. Belleville, Trenton, Cobourg, Port Hope, and Oshawa are all former lake ports.

Toronto and Hamilton, major commercial and industrial cities, have two of the largest harbours on the Great Lakes with opportunities for tours. The Toronto Islands have the oldest landmark in the city, the Gibraltar Point Lighthouse dating from 1809, which burned sperm whale oil in its first light. In Hamilton there are numerous sites with ship associations. There is the new Canada

Steamboats on the Lakes

Marine Discovery Centre operated by Parks Canada; HMCS *Haida*, a World War II destroyer; and Coots Paradise, located near the entrance to the Desjardin Canal.

Niagara-on-the-Lake is at the mouth of the mighty Niagara River and was a principal port during colonial times. Many 19th-century houses survive, the result of careful historic preservation. Information can be obtained at the Niagara Historical Society and Museum. The very successful Shaw Festival Theatre is located here.

Marine Museum of the Great Lakes at Kingston
55 Ontario Street
Kingston ON K7K 5P7
Tel: (613) 542-2261
Web site: http://www.marmus.ca/

Prince Edward County
Web site: http://www.quinte.on.ca/

Prince Edward County Chamber of Tourism & Commerce Office
116 Main Street
Picton ON
Tel: (613) 476-2421; toll free 1-800-640-4717

Gibraltar Point Lighthouse, Toronto Island
Web site: http://www.city.toronto.on.ca/parks/island/lighthouse.htm

Canada Marine Discovery Centre
57 Guise Street East
Hamilton ON L8L 8K4
Tel: (905) 526-0911
Web site: http://www.pc.gc.ca/canada/decouvertes_discovery/index_e.asp

HMCS *Haida* National Historic Site
Located at Pier 9, 658 Catharine Street North
Hamilton ON
Web site: http://hmcshaida.ca/

Niagara-on-the-Lake Chamber of Commerce and Visitor & Convention Bureau
This site links to the Niagara Historical Society and Museum.
Web site: http://www.niagaraonthelake.com/

Lake Erie

Drive along the Welland Canal road to Port Colborne, a town on Lake Erie that was created as the westerly terminus of the Welland Canal.

The shore road west along the north shore of Lake Erie is full of mystery and tight turns, but worth the extra navigation skills you will develop. Port Maitland, a former Royal Naval base, has a canal section. A few miles west is Port Dover with its fine Harbour Museum. Commercial fishing, once the dominant industry still, is still active. Many of the harbours you will pass through have impressive fishing fleets. Long Point and Point Pelee, the scenes of many shipwrecks, are nature reserves with well-designed interpretative features. At the end of Lake Erie and at the entrance to the Detroit River is Amherstburg. Fort Malden, a former British naval base there, is now a National Historic Site.

Port Dover Harbour Museum
44 Harbour Street
Port Dover ON N0A 1N0
Tel: (519) 583-2660
Web site: http://www.norfolkcounty.on.ca/Contribute/countyAdmin/departments/PortDoverHarbourMuseum.aspx

Long Point Provincial Park
Box 99
Rowan ON N0E 1M0
Tel: (519) 586-2133
Web site: http://www.ontarioparks.com/english/long.html#

Point Pelee National Park of Canada
407 Monarch Lane, R.R. 1
Leamington ON N8H 3V4
Phone: (519) 322-2365
Web site: http://www.pc.gc.ca/pn-np/on/pelee/index_e.asp

Fort Malden National Historic Site of Canada
P.O. Box 38, 100 Laird Avenue
Amherstburg ON N9V 2Z2
Tel: (519) 736-5416
Web site: http://www.pc.gc.ca/lhn-nhs/on/malden/index_e.asp

Detroit River, Windsor, Detroit, Lake St. Clair, Sarnia

It is a very busy waterway that connects Lake Erie to Lake Huron. The shore road from Amherstburg to Detroit and then along the St. Clair River will show you one of the great industrial centres of the United States — Detroit — and Canada at Sarnia.

I recommend a trip to the Henry Ford Museum and Greenfield Village, in Dearborn, Michigan, on the corner of Village Road and Oakwood Boulevard, just west of the Southfield Freeway (M-39) and south of Michigan Avenue (US-12). This is one of the outstanding museums of North America. It is here you will find some of the remaining James Watt engines collected by Henry Ford from England, and other examples of marine technology.

A Quick Tour of the Ontario Coastline of the Great Lakes

The Henry Ford Museum
20900 Oakwood Blvd.
Dearborn, MI 48124-4088
Tel: (313) 982-6100
Web site: http://www.hfmgv.org/museum/default.asp

LAKE HURON

Sarnia is a very good location for ship watchers, and it is here you can visit the beach enjoyed by passengers aboard the Northern Navigation Company ships noted in Chapter 7.

Goderich is still a Lakes ship port, shipping out salt, so head for the harbour, but be tempted on the way by the octagonal town square — a busy, joyful place. There is a maritime museum in the pilot house of the Lake freighter *Jay Morse* (1907) and a self-guided marine heritage walk that takes you to the flats where Goderich was founded and panoramic views of the harbour and Lake Huron.

Kincardine has a fine lighthouse dating from 1881 that was originally lit using kerosene, but now uses a 500-watt bulb. The port serviced the lumber, fishing, and salt industries.

Port Elgin and Southhampton are very close to each other and the centre of the marine history revivalist movement. There is a rare — for the Lakes — Imperial Lighthouse that can be visited on Chantry Island. The Chantry Island Institute, working with the Marine Heritage Society and the Bruce County Museum and Archives, offers lecture and activity programs.

We continue north and into the Bruce Peninsula. Stay with Highway 21 as long as you can before having to join the faster Highway 6.

Goderich Tourist Information Centre
Mailing address: 57 West Street, Goderich ON N7A 2K5
Location: 91 Hamilton Street, Goderich ON
Tel: (519) 524-6600 or toll free 1-800-280-7637
Web site: http://www.town.goderich.on.ca/visiting.html

Kincardine Visitor Information Centre
Corner of Hwy #9 & #21
Box 315, Kincardine ON N2Z 2Y8
Tel: (519) 396-2731; toll free 1-866-KIN-CRDN
Fax: (519) 396-7937
Web site: http://www.sunsets.com/kincardine/

Port Elgin Tourist Information
559 Goderich Street
Port Elgin ON N0H 2C4
Tel: (519) 832-2332, toll free 1-800-387-3456

Southampton Visitor's Centre
201 High Street
Southampton ON N0H 2L0
Tel: (519) 797-2215, toll free 1-888-757-2215
Web site: http://www.saugeenshores.ca/default2.asp

GEORGIAN BAY

Sometimes called the sixth Great Lake, Georgian Bay has everything a naturalist, camper, cyclist, or sailor could ask for: to the east, the Thirty Thousand Islands; to the south, world-renowned beaches; and on the western shore, a spectacular coastline with cliffs, walks, deep bays, and remote anchorages.

Tobermory is at the north end of the Bruce Peninsula. The village, an international destination objective for divers, is the base for Canada's first National Marine Conservation Area. The local waters include twenty-two shipwrecks and several historic lightstations. The freshwater ecosystem contains some of the most pristine waters of the Great Lakes. At Tobermory you can take a ferry to Manitoulin Island or continue south by road to Owen Sound.

There are museums with strong maritime collections at Owen Sound, Collingwood, Wasaga Beach, Penetanguishene, and Midland.

Own Sound, in a beautiful setting, had connections with Canadian Pacific Ships and is the first steel-shipbuilding site in Canada. It has the Owen Sound Marine & Rail Museum, housed in a former Canadian National Railway Station near the waterfront. The Museum's mission "is to bring people and history together." Owen Sound was named the Cultural Capital of Canada in 2004.

Collingwood Shipyard closed down in 1986. The lands are now under development, but the city and harbour are a part of our maritime history. On the Waterfront, the Watts boathouse survives from the days when the family were builders of watercraft used for fishing. The Collingwood Museum, with its strong maritime focus in a town shipping built, is a good place to start when visiting Collingwood.

Wasaga Beach, called the longest freshwater beach in the world, has a remarkable provincial museum that houses the remains of the schooner HMS *Nancy* dating from 1789. Stan Rogers immortalized the *Nancy* in his song of the same name.

Discovery Harbour at Penetanguishene, known to everyone as Penetang, has its origins in the early 19th century as a British Royal Navy base associated with the War of 1812 and due to the hard-working hydrographer Admiral Bayfield; the base has been re-created and can be toured. A short distance north is Midland, another important harbour.

Midland is in a beautiful setting with a main street that rolls down to the town dock — the place to be on an early summer's eve. There are marine history collections at Huronia Museum and Huron/Ouendat Village. Nearby is Sainte-Marie among the

Hurons, Ontario's first European community, established by the French Jesuits in 1639.

Parry Sound has a magnificent inner and outer harbour, and there are cruises that give you a flavour of the Thirty Thousand Islands and what the early navigators had to deal with in the days before electronics. An important classical musical festival, Festival of the Sound, takes place in a fine new performance centre. The best way to see the remarkable harbour and a portion of the Thirty Thousand Islands is to board a tour boat at Parry Sound.

As you move north on Highway 69 towards Sudbury you have the choice of making a digression on a smaller road to Killarney. Killarney is still relatively remote but treasured by those who have discovered it. Members of the Group of Seven, Frank Carmichael, Arthur Lismer, A.Y. Jackson, and A.J. Casson, all painted here and then lobbied with success for the creation of Killarney Park nearby. Baie Fine, what I would call a fiord, is a section of the park. The town was an important harbour for fishing and the timber industry.

Fathom Five National Marine Park
P.O. Box 189
Tobermory ON N0H 2R0
Administration: tel (519) 596-2233
Diver registration: tel (519) 596-2503
Web site: http://parkscanada.pch.gc.ca/amncnmca/on/fathomfive/index_e.asp

The Bruce Trail Association
The Association provides public access to the Niagara Escarpment while restoring its natural habitat. The Escarpment is a UNESCO World Biosphere Reserve.
Web site: http://www.brucetrail.org/

The Owen Sound Marine & Rail Museum
1155 1st Avenue West
Owen Sound ON N4K 4K8
Tel: (519) 371-3333
Web site: http://www.e-owensound.com/marinerail/

Collingwood Museum
Memorial Park, 45 St. Paul Street, Box 556
Collingwood ON L9Y 4B2
Tel: (705) 445-4811
Web site: www.town.collingwood.on.ca

The Friends of Nancy Island Historic Site
11-22nd Street North
Wasaga Beach ON L9Z 2V9
Tel: (705)429-2728 (Nancy Island) or (705) 429-2516 (office)
Web site: http://www.wasagabeachpark.com/war1812.html

Discovery Harbour
End of Jury Drive, Penetanguishene
Tel: (705) 549-8064
Web site: http://www.penetanguishene.ca/Attractions.cfm

Huronia Museum and Huron/Ouendat Village
549 Little Lake Park Road
Midland ON L4R 4P4
Tel: (705) 526-2844
Web site: http://www.huronmuseum.com

Town of Parry Sound
52 Seguin St.
Parry Sound ON P2A 1B4
Tel: (705) 746-2101
Web site: http://www.town.parry-sound.on.ca/

Killarney
Web sites: http://www.killarney.com/ and http://friendsofkillarneypark.ca/

THE MUSKOKA LAKES

A slight diversion from our Great Lakes coastline tour, the Muskoka Lakes offer a fully operating steamship, the *Segwun*. Visit Gravenhurst, the home port for this Royal Mailship built in 1889. The web site is particularly rich in content.

The Muskoka Lakes Hotel and Navigation Company
The Muskoka Fleet
820 Bay Street, Sagamo Park
Gravenhurst ON P1P 1G7
Tel: (705) 687-6667
Web site: http://www.segwun.com/

MANITOULIN ISLAND AND TOBERMORY

We are now returning to our coastline tour to board the 105-metre-long *Chi-Cheemaun* (which means "big canoe" in the Ojibwa language) at Tobermory and to cross the Main Channel between Georgian Bay and Lake Huron. This ferry crossing will give you a taste of the many natural dangers faced by 19th-century ships, both sailing and steam. Manitoulin Island is a magic place worthy of a generous allotment of time for visiting the villages and enjoying its many harbour views. Not to be forgotten is the passenger ship *Norisle* at Manitowaning. At the extreme west end of the Island is Meldrum Bay, where you will find the Net Shed Museum in a building formerly used by the commercial fishermen.

The *Chi-Cheemaun*
Web site with ferry schedule: http://www.tobermory.org/ferryservice.html

A Quick Tour of the Ontario Coastline of the Great Lakes

Manitoulin Island
This site links to local museums, including the Net Shed Museum and the *Norisle*.
Web site: http://www.manitoulin-island.com/

The North Channel

Leaving Manitoulin Island, turn west along the shore road, Highway 17, to visit some of the Turkey Trail ports noted in Chapter 4. There are good views of the North Channel, particularly further west. Take time to poke around town and to walk down to the docks. There are many diners where visitors can join the locals for good "Ontario" food. The route goes north to Sault Ste. Marie.

Lake Superior easily qualifies as an inland sea. Highway 17 north from the Soo to Thunder Bay is at times remote but rewarding. The scale is large and the views overlooking Lake Superior are the iconic Group of Seven images we all grew up with.

The harbours for Montreal River, Michipicoten River, Heron Bay, Marathon, Terrace Bay, Schreiber, Rossport, Nipigon, and Red Rock are off the main highway but never far away. Make a point of visiting these harbours, which played an important part in the commercial fishing, rail, and logging industries. It takes time to reconstruct those 19th-century harbours in your mind's eye, but in many cases the clues are there. Keep a lookout for Old Women Bay south of Wawa, which has a good site for swimming and picnicking at the base of the cliff just off the highway.

The city of Thunder Bay is the amalgamated communities of Fort William and Port Arthur. The early 20th-century shipyard is now known as Pascol Engineering. The drydock can accommodate 730-foot ships, and a few of the original Port Arthur Shipyard brick buildings remain. The Thunder Bay Historical Society and Museum has many marine-based collections. Fort William Historical Park is a re-creation dedicated to the commercial origins of the European settlement, the fur trade.

Lake Superior Provincial Park
P.O. Box 267
Wawa ON P0S 1K0
Tel: (705) 856-2284

The Friends of the Lake Superior Park
Web site: http://www.lakesuperiorpark.ca/

Individual Harbours
Visit the Canadian North Shore of Lake Superior Marina Guide at Web site http://www.lakesuperiorboating.com/main.htm

Thunder Bay Historical Museum Society
425 Donald Street East
Thunder Bay ON P7E 5V1
Tel: (807) 623-0801
Web site: http://www.thunderbaymuseum.com/

Fort William Historical Park
Follow Broadway Avenue off Hwy. 61 South
Thunder Bay ON
Tel: (807) 473-2344
Web site: http://www.fwhp.ca/

Sources

Ships

Beyond the information listed in the List of Ships section of this book, more detailed information about many of the steamships noted in the text can be derived from sources prepared by two remarkable men, the late Donald Page and John Mills. After a career spanning some forty years as a shipbuilder, Mr. Donald Page retired to Kingston. As the honorary curator of the Marine Museum of the Great Lakes, he documented the entire fleet of Canada Steamship Lines in great detail. Mr. John Mills laboured on his list for over three decades. His *Mills List* was first published by the Steamship Historical Society in 1979 with some 4,000 entries. In 1999 an updated and expanded list of over 6,000 entries was published by the Marine Museum of the Great Lakes at Kingston. *The New Mills List: Canadian Coastal and Inland Steam Vessels, 1809–1930* is available in a print edition through the Marine Museum, while both lists can be searched online and in full on the Museum web site at http://www.marmus.ca/. Follow the research links.

Know Your Ships: Guide to Boats and Boatwatching, Great Lakes and St. Lawrence Seaway, published by Marine Publishing Co. Inc., is the indispensable guide used by everyone from ship buffs to marine industry professionals. The Freshwater Press in Cleveland, Ohio, publishes other guides. A specialist who has been writing about Great Lakes shipping for decades is Skip Gillham, who, with collaborators, has published many titles. *The Ships of the Paterson Fleet*, written with Gene Onchulenko, is a good example; another is *Ships of Collingwood*.

Steamboats on the Lakes

RECOMMENDED READING

On the subject of steam there are hundreds of titles, but one recently published presents the subject in a very readable way: *Watt's Perfect Engine: Steam and the Age of Invention* by Ben Marsden. For a great collection of material on the early days of steam on the Great Lakes, try to find copies of the quarterly *FreshWater, A Journal of Great Lakes Marine History*, regrettably no longer published by the Marine Museum of the Great Lakes.

For more about Canadian canals, start with *Canals of Canada* and *Rideau Waterway* by Robert Legget. There are numerous titles on this topic, among the most recent being *A History of the Rideau Lockstations* by Ken W. Watson; *The Welland Canal* by Roberta M. Styran and Robert R. Taylor (well illustrated); and *The Welland Canal Company* by Hugh G. J. Aitken, a readable scholarly approach to the subject. A history of the waterway between Lake Ontario and Georgian Bay can be found in *Steamboating on the Trent-Severn* by Richard Tatley. The St. Lawrence River, Ottawa River, and Rideau system and canals are admirably treated in the very detailed and scholarly *Steamboat Connections: Montreal to Upper Canada, 1816–1843* by Frank Mackey.

Two older titles worth pursuing are *Pioneer Travel in Upper Canada* by Edwin C. Guillett and *Great Lakes Saga* by Anna G. Young. On the United States side of the Lakes there are more ports, people, and ships, and so Canadian content tends to be minimal in American publications. James P. Barry, in his *Ships of the Great Lakes*, has attempted to achieve a balance in telling his story.

For more on the Canadian Navy, a good start is *The Canadian Naval Chronicle: 1939–1945: The Successes and Losses of the Canadian Navy in World War II* by Captain Robert Darlington and Commander Fraser McKee. Nathan Greenfield has written an exciting and well-researched narrative, *The Battle of the St. Lawrence: The Second World War in Canada*. The battle of the convoys is well treated by Marc Milner in *North Atlantic Run*. Vanwell, a specialist publisher based in St. Catharines, has many other naval titles. For the most recent research, consider *The Northern Mariner*, a quarterly published by the Canadian Nautical Research Society.

For a good overview of labour history, try *Working Class Experience: Rethinking the History of Canadian Labour, 1800–1991* by Bryan D. Palmer. For a very detailed and absorbing narrative there is *Everything That Floats: Pat Sullivan, Hal Banks, and the Seamen's Unions of Canada* by William Kaplan.

Georgian Bay: The Sixth Great Lake and *Georgian Bay: An Illustrated History*, both by James Barry, who has a special interest in this area, are well worth having, while Richard Tatley has left no shoal uncovered with his *Northern Steamboats: Timiskaming, Nipissing and Abitibi, The Steamboat Era in the Muskokas, Volumes 1 and 2*. Many new regional titles are appearing, among them *The North Channel and St. Mary's River: A Guide to the History* by Andrea Gutsche, Barbara Chisholm, and Russell Floren; there are many more titles in this series.

Shipwrecks have attracted many authors, but a good place to start is with Cris Kohl and *Dive Ontario*, one of his many illustrated titles. Kohl's books include his sources, important to the diver and the marine historian.

THE WORLD WIDE WEB

There are numerous sites specializing in Great Lakes topics. The four web locations that follow are mature sites, rich in content, and they all have extensive links to other web-based sources of information.

- *Great Lakes and Seaway Shipping*, more commonly known as Boatnerd, at http://www.boatnerd.com/, is as popular with maritime professionals as it is with shipwatchers.
- A premier site at the entry- and advanced-research level is *The Marine History of the Great Lakes*, http://www.hhpl.on.ca/GreatLakes/, maintained by historian Walter Lewis.
- The *Association for Great Lakes Maritime History* is at http://www.aglmh.org/, with dozens of links to Lakes museums and historical societies.
- *The Marine Museum of the Great Lakes*, with its online ships lists and catalogue entries for the research library, as well as ships drawings and archives, is a good entry for Canadian research at http://www.marmus.ca.

Index

able seamen, 60
Accommodation, 18, 19, 82
Adelaide, 22, 36, 82
A.E. Ames, 54, 82
Alberta, 41, 82
Alciope, 22, 82
Alexander, Lincoln, 50
Algoma, 41, 82
Algoma Central Corporation, 42, 63
Algoma Central Marine, 75, 76, 77
Algoma Central Railway, 42
Algoma Steel, 42
"alligator" (amphibious) vessels, 46, 59
America, 25, 82
American Civil War, 25
Amherstburg, 90
Angstrom, A., 53
Angus, Bruce, 58
Asia, 39, 82
Assiniboia, 37, 41, 70, 82
Athabasca/Athabaska, 41, 82

Banks, Hal, 74
Barge *137,* 58, 82
Bark, Wilfrid, 63–65
Beauharnois Canal, 88
Beeton, Horace, 67
Belleville, 54, 82
Bennett & Henderson, 22
Bertram Engine Works Company Ltd., 53
Bessemer process, 42
Bethune, Donald, 24–27
Blue Cross, 58, 82
bosuns, 60
Boulton, Mathew, 10
Boulton and Watt engine, 18, 22
Brashear, John, 79
Britannia, 24–25, 82
British trade policy, 16–17
By, John, 32

cabins, 21–22, 23
Cambria. See *Champion*
Canada (1826), 23, 25, 82
Canada (1841), 82
Canada Marine Discovery Centre, 89–90
Canada Steamship Lines (CSL), 52, 53, 54, 57, 59, 62, 63, 65, 67, 68, 75, 76
Canadian Beaver, 57, 82
Canadian Dredge and Dock, 59
Canadian Farmer, 57
Canadian General Electric, 76
Canadian Government Merchant Marine, 56
Canadian Leader, 76–77, 82
Canadian Navigation Company, 52
Canadian Pacific Railway, 41, 43, 52
Canadian Provider, 76, 82
Canadian Rover, 57, 83

Canadian Seaman's Union (CSU), 61, 62, 72
canals, 9, 29, 30, 32, 33–34, 38, 47, 48, 58, 70–71, 88
captain, 60, 61
Carillon Canal, 32
Car of Commerce, 18, 19, 83
Caspian, 54, 83
Cayuga, 54, 66, 68–69, 83
Champion, 83
Chantler family, 33
Chapman, James, 19
Charlotte, 20, 21, 83
Chi-Cheemaun, 92
Chickluna Shipyard, 25
Chicora, 37, 38, 83
Chief Justice Robinson, 25, 83
Chippewa, 54, 55, 83
cholera outbreak, 33
Churchill, Winston, 72
City of Hamilton, 25, 83
City of Kingston, 24, 83
City of Toronto, 83
Clergue, Francis, 41–42
Clermont, 10, 83
Clevelands House, 49
Cobourg, 33, 83
Cockburn, Alexander Peter, 47–48, 49
Colborne, Sir John, 33
Collingwood, 38, 43
Collingwood Shipyards, 58, 59, 91
Columbian, 83
Commerce, 25, 83
Commodore Barrie, 24, 83
compasses, magnetic, 36, 40
compounding, 31
Consolidated Lake Superior Company, 42
containerization, 75
cook, 60
cook's helpers, 60
Coulter, John, 78
Coverdale, 68, 83
Coverdale, William H., 68

Davis Drydock, 59, 79
D.D. Calvin, 83
D.D. Calvin & Co., 53
decorum, 21–22
Dickens, Charles, 27
Discovery Harbour, 91
Donald Stewart, 65, 83
D.R. Van Allen, 83
Dufferin, Lord, 39
Durham boats, 31, 33, 83

Edmonton, 70, 83–84
Elder, Jim, 75
engineers, 59, 60
Erie Canal, 29, 34
Erin, 43, 84
Eugene C. Roberts, 84

Europa, 30, 84

Family Compact, 28
Faucille canal, 88
Fort Malden, 90
Fort William, 42–43
Fort William Historical Park, 93
Frank A. Sherman, 84
Frank B. Baird, 65, 84
Frankcliffe Hall, 77, 84
Frontenac, 10, 17, 19–22, 24, 36, 84

Georgian Bay, 39–40, 47
Georgian Bay Ship Canal, proposed, 47
Gibraltar Point Lighthouse, 89
Gildersleeve, Henry, 20, 21, 24–27, 26
Gildersleeve House, 89
Glencorrie, 84
Glencova, 52, 84
Gleneagles, 53, 84
Gleniffer, 52, 84
Glenlinnie, 84
Glenmohr, 84
Goderich, 58
Goldby, Tom, 64
grain trade, 58
Gravenhurst, 48, 49, 78–79
Great Britain, 22–23, 25, 32, 84
Great Lakes, 15
barriers to travel, 14, 17
cruises, 62–63
sailing conditions, 24
shipwrecks, 12–13
surveyed, 14
Upper Lakes, 37–45
Great Lakes Navigation Company, 52
Great Lakes Power Company, 42
Great Lakes schooner, 17, 30
Great Northern Transit Company, 39
Greenfield Village, 90

Haida, 90
Halifax, 77, 84
Hamilton, John, 22, 23, 25
Hamilton (city), industrial expansion, 51
Hamonic, 45, 54, 62–63, 67–68, 84
Henry Ford Museum, 90
Hochelaga, 68, 84
Holden, Mary, 31
horse ferry, 18
Howard, Alan, 66–67, 68
Howard L. Shaw, 74, 84
Howison, John, 21
Hudson Bay, 15
Huronia Museum and Huron/Ouendat Village, 91
Huronic, 54, 84

immigration, 27, 31–33
Inter-Ocean, 46, 84
investors, 18, 30

James Bay, 15
James Norris, 76, 85
James Swift, 85
James Whalen, 85
Jay Morse, 91
J.H. Plummer, 54, 85
John B. Richards, 58, 85
John S. Pillsbury, 85
J.T. Reid & Sons, 58

Kaczkowski, Viktor, 75
Keewatin, 41, 45, 70, 85
Killarney, 92
Kincardine, 91
Kingston, 9, 19, 53, 68, 85
Kingston (city), 18, 59, 79–80
Kingston Shipyards, 58, 63
Kirby, Frank E., 53

labour movement, 60–62, 72–75
Lachine Canal, 30, 33, 88
La Compagnie du Richelieu, 52
Lady Colborne, 36, 85
Lake Erie
shipwrecks, 12–13
waters, 35–36
Lake Huron, shipwrecks, 13
Lake Nipissing, 46, 47
Lake Ontario, shipwrecks, 12
Lake Superior, shipwrecks, 13
Lake Temiskaming, 46, 47
Laurier, Sir Wilfrid, 47
Lawrence, John, 72
Leitch, Gordon, 58
Leitch, Jack, 74
LeMoyne, 59, 70
See also *Glenmohr*
Leys, John, 24
lighthouses, 36
log line, 40
Long Point, 12, 36, 90
lookout, 40
Lord Sydenham, 23, 85

Macassa, 54, 85
Macdonald, Sir John A., 27, 39
Maggie Hunter, 14, 85
Magnet, 23, 28, 85
Majestic, 38, 85
Malsham, 19, 85
Manitoba, 37, 41, 64, 85
Manitoulin, 44–45
Manitoulin Island, 92
Mann, Gother, 32
Maple Leaf, 25, 85
Maritime Workers Union of the Great Lakes, 61
Mathewston, 85
Mattawan, 46, 85
McMaster, Newbold, 61
Merchants Mutual Line, 54
mergers and takeovers, 52, 53

Merritt, William Hamilton, 34
Metal Craft Marine, 59
Midland Navigation Company, 52
Midland Shipyards, 52, 59
Modjeska, 54, 85
Molson, John, 18, 19
Montreal, 53, 85
Montrealais, 76, 85
Montreal Transportation Company, 54
Morden, Grant, 52
Morrison, Christy Anne, 39
Morton, Desmond, 74
Muir Drydock, 59
Museum of the Great Lakes, 89
Muskoka and Nipissing Navigation Company, 46–50
Muskoka Lakes Navigation Company, 47
Muskoka Steamship and Historical Society, 78

Nancy, 91
National Seamen's Association, 61
navigation instruments, 40
Net Shed Museum, 92
Newcomen, Thomas, 10
New Era, 86
Niagara, 22
Niagara Falls, 15, 34
Niagara Navigation Company, 52, 53
Niagara-on-the-Lake, 90
Nipissing, 49, 77, 86
Nipissing/Segwun, 77, 78, 86
Norgoma, 89
Noronic, 54, 62–63, 86
Noronic fire, 45, 66–67
Norris, James, 58
Norseman, 86
North Channel, 43, 44, 93
Northern Navigation Company, 54
North King, 54
See also *Norseman*
Northland Steamship Company, 58
Northumberland, 67, 86
Northwest Rebellion, 38

Ontario, 20, 86
Ontario Road Builders Association, 78
Operation Torch, 64
Ottawa River, 15
Owen Sound, 41, 59
Owen Sound Marine & Rail Museum, 91

paddlewheel steamer, 11–12, 30
Page, Donald A., 53
Pascol Engineering, 76
Passport, 23, 86
Paterson, N.M., 57
Paterson Steamships Limited, 57, 63, 65
Pathfinder (1921), 53, 86
Pathfinder (1963), 86
Phoebe, 79–80, 86
Playfair, James, 52–53, 58, 59
Ploughboy, 39, 86
Point Pelee, 12, 36, 90

Polson Yard, 59
Portadoc, 65
See also *Eugene C. Roberts*
Port Arthur, 42–43
Port Arthur Shipyards, 43, 58, 63, 93
Port Colborne Historical and Marine Museum and Heritage Village, 89
Port Dalhousie, 89
Port Dover, 90
Port Maitland, 90
Port McNichol, 41
Portsmouth Village, 89
Port Weller Shipyards, 59, 70, 76
Press Association of Canada, 49
Prince Arthur's Landing, 37
Prince Edward County, 12, 89
Prince of Wales, 24, 86
propeller propulsion, 30–31
Prospect House, 49
Pump House Steam Museum, 79

Quebec, 68, 86
Quebecois, 76, 86
Queen Charlotte, 86
Queen Victoria, 25, 86

Racine, 38
See also *City of Toronto*
railways, 15, 38, 48
Ralph Budd, 58, 86
Rapids Prince, 53, 86
Rapids Queen, 53
See also *Columbian*
Rebellion of 1837, 28
Red River Rebellion, 27
resource economy, 38, 42–43, 46–48
Revenge, 55, 87
Richardson, Hugh, 25, 26–27
Richelieu & Ontario Navigation Company, 48, 52, 53
Rideau Canal, 9, 30, 31, 32, 88
Riel, Louis, 37, 38
"rigolet" canal, 88
Robert Fulton, 18
Rosseau House, 49
Royal Muskoka Hotel, 49
Russel Brothers, 59

sagging, 13
sailing ships, 13–14, 17, 28–29, 30
sailors
training of, 13, 63–64
working and living conditions, 60–61
Sainte-Marie among the Hurons, 91–92
St. Catharines Museum, 89
St. George, 32, 87
St. Lawrence Canal, 24, 58
St. Lawrence River, 15, 30
St. Lawrence River Steam Navigation Company, 52
St. Lawrence Seaway, 58, 59, 70–71, 88
Salsberg, Joe, 61
Sarnia, 91
Sarnian, 87
Sault Ste. Marie, 37, 38, 51, 62, 63
Scotch boiler, 46

Scott Misner Steamships, 63
Seafarers International Union (SIU), 72, 74–75
Seaway Bulk Carriers, 77
Segwun, 50, 77, 78, 79, 87
sextant, 40
Shaw, Gordon, 44
ship owning, 24–27, 52–54, 75
Shipping Federation of Canada, 72
shipping industry
bulk cargo, 38–39, 70, 75
Cold War and, 72–75
Great Depression, 57–63
labour and safety laws, 67, 70
mergers and acquisitions in, 52, 53
passenger trade, 21–22, 23, 45, 62–63, 68–70
price wars, 25
technological change, 10–11, 24, 30, 75
shipwrecks, 12–13, 14
shipyards, 19, 24, 47–48, 54–55, 56, 58–59, 63, 70, 76
Silver Islet, 43
Simcoe. See *Glencorrie*
Sir James Dunn, 68, 87
Smith, Henry, 39
Soulanges Canal, 60, 88
Spartan, 87
square sails, 17
Stadacona, 87
steam engine, 10–11, 24, 75
steamships
crew, 45, 59–60
elegance and comfort of, 21–22, 23, 45, 62–63
fires, 66–68
navigation instruments, 40
and northern communities, 43–45
reliability of, 14
repairs, 48
and resource economy, 38, 42–43, 48–49
wood ships, 13
steam turbine, 11
steam turbine engine, 75
Stedman, John, 31–32
steerage class, 22
steward, 60
stokers, 59–60
Stormount, 54, 87
Sullivan, Pat, 61–62
Swiftsure, 18, 19, 87

Teabout, Henry, 19
telegraph service, 9
Telgeman, Jack, 79
TEU (twenty-foot equivalent unit), 75
Thirty Thousand Islands, 92
Thoms, Stuart, 75
Thousand Island Steamboat Company, 52
Thunder Bay, 51
See also Fort William; Port Arthur
Thunder Bay, 68
See also *Stadacona*

Thunder Bay Historical Society and Museum, 93
timber industry, 48–49
Tinkiss, Dukan, 39
Tobermory, 91
Toronto (1825), 33, 87
Toronto (1898), 53, 55, 87
Toronto Islands, 89
tourism, 48–50
T.R. McLagan, 87
Transit (Constitution), 25, 87
trawlers, 55, 87
Trent Severn Canal, 88
Trou-du-Moulin canal, 88
Trudeau, Pierre, 78
Turbinia, 53, 87
Turkey Trail ports, 44, 93

U-boats, 65
United Kingdom, 32
See also *Alciope*
"up," in maritime usage, 88
Upper Canada
communication links, 9–10, 15, 29–30
defence, 32
economic rivalry with US, 16–17, 19, 29, 34–35
self-government, 28
Upper Great Lakes, 63, 65
Upper Lakes and St. Lawrence Transportation Company Ltd., 58
Upper Lakes Shipping, 74, 76, 77

Van Allen, 57
Venetia, 53, 87

walking beam engine, 11, 30
Walk-in-the-Water, 29, 35, 87
Wanda III, 87
Ward, John Dod, 20
Wasaga Beach, 91
watercraft, 49–50
Watt, James, 10
Watts boathouse, 91
Waubuno, 39–40, 87
Welland Canal, 9, 15, 30, 34, 47, 58, 59, 70, 71, 88
Wenona, 47–48, 87
Westmount, 54, 87
Wevers, Henk, 80
Weyburn, 63–64, 65, 87
wheelsmen, 60
William IV, 24, 87
Windermere House, 49
wipers, 59, 60
World War I, Great Lakes shipyards in, 54–55
World War II
losses, 63–64
shipbuilding, 63

Ypres, 55, 87